Praying the Liturgy of th
Father Timothy Gallagher
a priest who discovers the power and promise of the Breviary. Both veterans of the Divine Office and newcomers alike will be inspired and encouraged by his humble journey of faith. Particularly helpful is the discussion of the Divine Office as a relational prayer of praise. Here, Father Gallagher artfully shows how praying the Liturgy of the Hours is never a private act, but one that intimately unites us to Jesus and His Church. I warmly recommend this book to anyone—clergy, religious, or laity—who wishes to pray the Liturgy of the Hours with greater attentiveness and devotion.

—Timothy Michael Cardinal Dolan,
Archbishop of New York

Fr. Timothy Gallagher's willingness to present candidly his own struggles with the psalms makes *Praying the Liturgy of the Hours: A Personal Journey* immediately helpful to all those who desire to pray the Liturgy of the Hours with more spiritual profit.

Francis Cardinal George,
Archbishop of Chicago

Father Gallagher writes a captivating account on the spiritual richness found in the Liturgy of the Hours. The faithful who have experienced praying with the psalms to be a challenge will be helped by Father Gallagher's humble admission of his own personal difficulties with this ancient form of prayer. As Father Gallagher unlocks the depth of the Divine Office, the reader is led to understand and embrace this prayer of the Church with a renewed sense of appreciation and awe.

—Donald Cardinal Wuerl, Archbishop of Washington

Father Gallagher has described an unfolding appreciation for the Liturgy of the Hours that names the experience of so many of us who have prayed the Hours for years. The growing number of those who are just beginning to know this prayer of the Church hear in these pages an invitation to be formed daily as prayerful disciples of Jesus Christ. We can all be grateful for this encouragement to reflect more deeply on the gift of the Liturgy of the Hours.

—Most Reverend George Lucas,
Archbishop of Omaha, NE

Fr. Gallagher's book, *Praying the Liturgy of the Hours: A Personal Journey,* stirred my interest right away and kept me fully engaged from beginning to end. Efforts to study the psalms and to understand how the Hours draw us into the life of Christ and the Church are needed from time to time, and always bring wonderful benefits for mind and heart. This is where Fr. Gallagher's book makes a real contribution. I heartily endorse *Praying the Liturgy of the Hours: A Personal Journey* and recommend it in particular for priests and religious, and for all those who want to grow closer to Jesus in their daily lives.

—Most Reverend Thomas Olmstead,
Bishop of Phoenix, AZ

In this thoughtful and well-crafted book, Fr. Timothy Gallagher provides some very helpful clarification regarding the theology and spirituality that inform the Liturgy of the Hours. But his greatest contribution is the sharing of his personal struggles with the "office" over many years. His honest and searching self-examination will prove invaluable to anyone who has undertaken the responsibility of praying this great prayer of the Church.

—Father Robert Barron, rector of Mundelein
Seminary and author of *Catholicism:
A Journey to the Heart of the Faith, Word on Fire:
Proclaiming the Power of Christ,* and others

Both the newcomer to the Liturgy of the Hours, and those of us who have been praying the Office for years, will be genuinely enriched by this "personal journey." For the person wrestling with the recitation of the Hours, I believe that Fr. Gallagher's words of encouragement offer an impetus to renewal and a more profound relationship with Christ through the perennial prayer of the Church. In my own heart I feel a movement from the temptation of complacency of habit to a renewed desire to delve deeply and receive richly from this treasury of grace.

—Rev. Msgr. David L. Toups, S.T.D., rector of St. Vincent de Paul Regional Seminary, Boynton Beach, FL

As a priest of fifty-four years with multiple responsibilities in pastoral ministry, habit and over-familiarity unconsciously have led me down an uneven and at times bumpy path of simply "*saying*" the Divine Office. Father Gallagher attracted me by the very title of his book, *Praying the Liturgy of the Hours*. He tells us of his personal journey but only to prompt us to reflect meaningfully upon our own particular journeys into praying the Liturgy of the Hours. I highly recommend this book as a welcome travelogue into new discoveries of beauty in the word of God and wellsprings of nourishment that we may have missed along a well-worn path that we have all trod and that we continue to travel.

—Msgr. John A. Cippel, retired pastor of the Diocese of St. Petersburg, FL, and spiritual director, St. John Vianney College Seminary, Miami, FL

The Liturgy of the Hours is an "experience of spiritual growth." Father Gallagher demonstrates this reality by providing us with his own experience of appreciating this "ancient but ever new" Prayer of the Church. The reader of this text will be able to resonate with Father Gallagher's own stages and development of prayer. With very practical examples of growth, this book will be of help to all who desire to pray the Liturgy of the Hours with greater devotion and attentiveness.

—Rev. Gregory J. Hoppough, C.S.S., professor of liturgy,
Pope St. John XXIII National Seminary, Weston, MA

I have prayed the Liturgy of the Hours for over forty years, and Father Gallagher has helped me find new depths in it, as well as offering paths to other ways of enriching this form of prayer. His sharing of his own journey and challenges in praying the Liturgy of the Hours is encouraging. I also appreciate that he gives witness to the fruitfulness of this ancient prayer of the Church for laypersons.

—Sister Linda Sevcik, S.M., regional leader, Marist Sisters

Father Gallagher's honesty and ability to describe the joys and the challenges he faces as he perseveres with this spiritual practice are very inspiring and refreshing. I would recommend this book to anyone who wishes to engage fully in any Christian spiritual practice, as his insights touch on the same kind of experiences that most people face in their daily prayer. Delight, struggles to continue, boredom, and peace: these are all words to describe what happens to anyone who desires a continued relationship with God through prayer. Father Gallagher lives them all.

—Elizabeth Koessler, spiritual director, wife, and mother

In Father Timothy Gallagher's book we listen to his personal and heartfelt struggles in saying the Liturgy of the Hours. He offers us workable techniques and suggestions that will help us learn not only to "say" the Hours, but to "pray" with them so as to make God's holy Word our own. This book is a gift to priests and laity alike. Read it as you pray the Liturgy of the Hours. You will not be disappointed.

—Lawrence A. Dwyer, husband and attorney-at-law

Praying the Liturgy of the Hours

Praying the Liturgy of the Hours

A Personal Journey

TIMOTHY M. GALLAGHER, O.M.V.

A Crossroad Book
The Crossroad Publishing Company
www.crossroadpublishing.com

© 2014 by Timothy M. Gallagher, O.M.V.
Printed in 2014.

Crossroad, Herder & Herder, and the crossed C logo/colophon are trademarks
of The Crossroad Publishing Company.

Library of Congress Cataloging-in-Publication Data available from the Library
of Congress.

ISBN 978-08245-2032-8

Cover design by: George Foster
Book design by: Scribe Inc.

Books published by The Crossroad Publishing Company may be purchased
at special quantity discount rates for classes and institutional use. For
information, please e-mail info@crossroadpublishing.com.

Printed in the United States of America.

Contents

Acknowledgments

I am deeply grateful to the many who assisted me in the writing of this book: in particular, to Father Gregory Hoppough, C.S.S., and Sister Mary Timothea Elliot, R.S.M., for their help with theological and liturgical considerations and for their reading of the manuscript; to Claire-Marie Hart, who once again generously assisted me with her editorial wisdom; to those who read and offered comments on the manuscript, Teresa Monaghen, A.O., Father Nicholas Cachia, Msgr. John Cippel, Sister Linda Sevcik, S.M., Father Gregory Short, O.M.V., Larry Dwyer, Elizabeth Koessler, Lee McDowell, Msgr. Gregory Schlesselmann, James Gallagher, and Richard McKinney; to Carol McGinness for her aid with the practicalities of publication; to the editor, Jane Cavolina, for her guidance in preparing the manuscript; and to all at Crossroad for their assistance and support throughout this process. To each I am most grateful.

Finally, I thank the following for permission to reprint copyrighted material:

Scripture texts in this work are taken from the *New American Bible, Revised Edition* © 2010, 1991, 1986, 1970 Confraternity of Christian Doctrine, Washington, D.C., and are used by permission of the copyright owner. All rights reserved. No part of the New American Bible may be reproduced in any form without permission in writing from the copyright owner.

Revised Standard Version Bible—Second Catholic Edition (Ignatius Edition) Copyright © 2006 National Council

Praying the Liturgy of the Hours

Introduction

I HAD JUST CELEBRATED the noon Mass in the Catholic student center where I was to speak that evening. I left the sacristy and returned to the church. A number of students had remained after the Mass, and others were entering. Soon, a group of fifteen was gathered in the pews on the right, facing the altar.

I knew they were about to pray Daytime Prayer from the Liturgy of the Hours. I had heard that these students prayed the Liturgy of the Hours together and was interested to witness their prayer. I joined them, and Daytime Prayer began. Some used the book of the Liturgy of the Hours; others recited the text from their smartphones.

The students sang the three psalms of Daytime Prayer with tones they obviously knew well. The melodies were simple, and several sang in harmony, at times in three voices. I was totally unprepared for the depth, simplicity, and reverence of their prayer. I had said Daytime Prayer for forty years and had never heard it prayed so warmly and richly, with a beauty I found captivating. I felt as though I were discovering it for the first time. I had always thought Daytime Prayer to be simply a brief prayer at midday; now I experienced it as a nourishing and faith-filled encounter with the Lord in the heart of the day's activity. And these were university students, stopping to pray in the midst of their classes!

After the psalms, a student approached the lectern for the reading from Scripture and proclaimed it unhurriedly, from the heart. The entire prayer lasted ten to fifteen minutes. When it concluded, most of the students left. Some stayed to pray on their own.

At 6:00 P.M., I returned for Evening Prayer. This time, about thirty students participated, again using printed or electronic texts. A leader accompanied the psalms on the piano, and another student guided the singing from the microphone. Once more, the tones were simple and attractive, with occasional harmonizing, especially for the Magnificat, Mary's canticle of praise. Here, too, I sensed the prayerful quality I had felt in Daytime Prayer.

The next day, I missed no opportunity to pray the Liturgy of the Hours with the students. Thirty joined in Morning Prayer. One served as cantor and another as lector. Again the singing was inviting, reverent, and prayerful. That evening, forty-five gathered for Evening Prayer, and at 10:30 P.M., twenty for Night Prayer. The leader told me that they had begun to pray the Liturgy of the Hours six months earlier and that attendance was quietly growing.

I had never seen anything like this: university students praying the Liturgy of the Hours, once, twice, and more times a day, and praying it with such simplicity and beauty. The student center offered these young men and women—and the older persons who joined them—not only the option of daily Mass but also a means of praying together *throughout the entire day.*

Can the Liturgy of the Hours, with its hymns, psalms, readings, and intercessions, become the prayer of *every* Christian—priest, religious, and layperson? Can it bring new energy into our spiritual lives? Should we consider adopting it? Should *I* consider adopting it? All of it? Part of it? If we already pray it, can we be renewed in this prayer? Learn more about it? Find ways to pray it with greater richness?

I began praying the Liturgy of the Hours forty years ago. In this book, I will share that experience. I will review both the struggles and the blessings the Liturgy of the Hours has brought into my life. There is nothing extraordinary about my story. I share it precisely because it is so *ordinary*—personal, yes, in its nuances, but for the rest, I am sure, much like the experience of many who pray the Liturgy of the Hours.

Over the years, I have come to believe that ordinary spiritual experience is the most important. Peak moments occur a few times in our lives. In general, however, the spiritual life consists of ordinary experience with its daily joys and struggles, daily efforts to pray, and daily striving to love God and others. How we live this "ordinary" experience determines everything in our relationship with God.

I have spent much of the past three decades teaching and writing about Ignatian discernment of spirits.[1] This ministry has taught me that when ordinary spiritual experience is expressed in words, new paths open in our lives of faith. Saint Ignatius's teaching on discernment, for example, assists us most when presented through ordinary spiritual experience: a man driving home from work with anxiety in his heart; a woman rising in the morning, joyfully aware of God's closeness; a parishioner at daily Mass seeking God's help in a time of discouragement . . . people in the midst of ordinary activity, following the guidance of the Spirit and rejecting the desolations of the enemy.[2] When discernment is so presented, a person says, "Now I see what this teaching means. Now I understand how this can help me. Now I can apply this in my life."

The same is true of the Liturgy of the Hours. When the ordinary experience of praying the Liturgy of the Hours is described in words, this prayer no longer appears remote, a practice reserved to a few, but becomes possible for all. Struggles, too, in this prayer, when shared, weigh less. And above all, the fruit of this prayer, when expressed, strengthens hope.

Every spiritual story is individual. Mine is necessarily shaped by my vocation as a religious and priest and by my specific circumstances of place, time, and personality. None of this is universal! I believe, however, that most of the struggles and blessings experienced in praying the Liturgy of the Hours are common to all. It is my hope that describing these struggles and blessings in the concreteness of an individual story will encourage others who pray, or may decide to pray, the Liturgy of the Hours.

Writing on the history, theology, and rubrics of the Liturgy of the Hours exists.[3] This is a book on the *experience* of praying the Liturgy of the Hours and of praying it over many years. Hundreds of thousands of priests, religious, and laypeople pray the Liturgy of the Hours. Those who pray it in part may dedicate ten to fifteen minutes a day to it; those who pray the entire Liturgy of the Hours devote to it an hour or more *every day* of their lives. In terms of time alone, this is a significant part of life. When we consider the potential of the Liturgy of the Hours for spiritual growth, that significance deepens beyond measure. The Liturgy of the Hours is a part of life, an experience of prayer that merits our explicit attention and reflection.

I write this book for all who pray the Liturgy of the Hours. I write it also for all who may desire to undertake this prayer, in part or in whole. The Second Vatican Council taught with great emphasis that the Liturgy of the Hours is a prayer for the *entire* people of God. May it be for us, as for those university students, a rich source of spiritual growth.

Prologue

What Is the Liturgy of the Hours?

My psalter is my joy.
—Saint Augustine

SINCE THE OLD TESTAMENT times when they were written, people of faith have loved the Psalms. Devout Jews turned to these one hundred fifty prayers in times of joy and sorrow, of peace and desperate need. Jesus knew, quoted, and prayed the Psalms; in him, the fullness of divine revelation, the Psalms acquired their deepest meaning.[1] The early Christians likewise prayed them and, when the persecutions of the first centuries ceased, gathered for this prayer in their churches.

In the Psalms, they found prayers of confidence in God: "The Lord is my shepherd; there is nothing I shall want. . . . If I should walk in the valley of darkness, no evil would I fear. You are there with your crook and your staff" (Ps 23:1).[2] Through the Psalms, like Jesus, they cried to God in times of affliction: "My God, my God, why have you forsaken me? You are far from my plea and the cry of my distress" (Ps 22:2). With the words of the Psalms, they expressed hope in God: "The Lord is my light and my help; whom shall I fear? The Lord is the stronghold of my life; before whom shall I shrink?" (Ps 27:1); and deep longing for God: "Like the deer that yearns for running streams, so my soul is yearning for you, my God" (Ps 42:1). When they had strayed and sought conversion, the Psalms supplied the prayers they needed: "Have mercy on me, God, in your kindness. In your compassion blot out my offense" (Ps 51:3). And when their hearts rejoiced in God, again the Psalms provided the words: "My soul, give praise to the Lord; I will praise the Lord all my days, make music to my God while I live" (Ps 146:1–2).

A psalm, wrote Saint Ambrose, is "a cry of happiness." A psalm, he continued, "soothes the temper, distracts from care, lightens the burden of sorrow. It is a source of security at night, a lesson of wisdom by day. It is a shield when we are afraid, a celebration of holiness, a vision of serenity, a promise of peace and harmony." "Day," Saint Ambrose affirmed, "begins to the music of a psalm, [and] day closes to the echo of a psalm."[3]

Saint Athanasius declared that "the psalms seem to me to be like a mirror, in which the person using them can see himself, and the stirrings of his own heart; he can recite them against the background of his own emotions."[4] Saint Augustine expressed his joy in hearing the psalms sung: "How I wept when I heard your hymns [psalms] and canticles, being deeply moved by the sweet singing of your Church. Those voices flowed into my ears, truth filtered into my heart, and from my heart surged waves of devotion. Tears ran down, and I was happy in my tears."[5]

Throughout the Church, in Palestine, Antioch, Constantinople, and Africa, Christians gathered in their churches twice each day to pray the psalms.[6] Daily they assembled for "morning and evening hymns," as these services were known. If a bishop was present, he would lead; if not, a priest. The people sang the morning and evening psalms, unvaried and so known by heart. Other biblical and non-biblical canticles might be added. In some places, a homily would be given. The services ended with intercessions and a prayer by the bishop or priest.[7]

With the passage of centuries, the prayer of the psalms passed into the monasteries. These absorbed almost completely the earlier "people's office," a vestige of which remained in Sunday evening Vespers in parishes.[8] In monasticism, other "hours" were added to the morning and evening services, and monks prayed the psalms in the early morning, repeatedly during the day, and before retiring at night.[9] Thus arose the "Divine Office," the "holy task," the "sacred duty" of praying the psalms throughout the day and night to fulfill the scriptural ideal of ceaseless prayer (Lk 18:1; 1Thes 5:17).[10]

In the renewal following the Second Vatican Council, the term "Divine Office" was retained and continues to be used. The more specific "Liturgy of the Hours" replaced it, however, as the preferred title.[11] This daily prayer of the psalms, with its added hymns, readings, and invocations, belongs to the Church's liturgy—her official, public prayer. Like the Mass and the other sacraments—baptism, confirmation, reconciliation, marriage, holy orders, and the anointing of the sick—the *Liturgy* of the Hours is liturgical prayer.

The Liturgy of the Hours differs, however, from other liturgical prayer precisely as a prayer *of the hours*. The Mass, for example, though unparalleled in its spiritual richness, is celebrated at one moment in the day; the Liturgy of the Hours provides liturgical prayer throughout the entire day: morning, midday, evening, and night.[12] It is the Church's greatest gift to hearts that long for prayerful communion with God throughout the day.

This prayer is for *all* in the Church. Priests and deacons pray the Liturgy of the Hours by mandate of the Church and religious according to the directives of their constitutions. "The laity, too," Vatican II taught, "are encouraged to recite the Divine Office, either with the priests, or among themselves, or even individually."[13] The postconciliar Church urged families to pray the Liturgy of the Hours: "It is desirable that the family . . . should not only pray together to God but should also celebrate some parts of the Liturgy of the Hours as occasion offers, so as to enter more deeply into the life of the Church."[14] Looking to the third millennium, Pope John Paul II declared that the Liturgy of the Hours is "warmly recommended to lay people."[15] Pope Benedict XVI expressed a similar desire: "I would then like to renew to you all the invitation to pray with the Psalms, even becoming accustomed to using the Liturgy of the Hours of the Church, Morning Prayer in the morning, Evening Prayer in the evening, and Night Prayer before retiring."[16]

The complete Liturgy of the Hours fills four volumes disposed according to the Church's liturgical year: Volume One, the Advent and Christmas seasons; Volume Two, the Lenten and Easter Seasons; Volumes Three and Four, the thirty-four weeks of Ordinary Time.[17] These volumes contain the psalms, distributed over a four-week repeating cycle, and their accompanying hymns, antiphons, biblical readings, intercessions, and texts for the Office of Readings. The volumes also provide prayers and readings specific to the seasons, solemnities, feasts, and memorials of saints in the Church's liturgical year.[18] Electronic and shorter printed versions abound, rendering the Liturgy of the Hours widely accessible.[19]

The renewed Liturgy of the Hours offers five daily times of prayer: Morning Prayer, to be said as the day begins; Daytime Prayer, to be said in late morning, midday, or midafternoon; Evening Prayer, to be said in the evening; Night Prayer, to be said just before retiring; and the Office of Readings, a longer and more meditative prayer to be said at any convenient time during the day. Morning and Evening Prayer, depending on how they are prayed—alone or in a group, with or without singing, and so forth—may take ten to fifteen minutes. Daytime Prayer is shorter and Night Prayer shorter still. The Office of Readings may take twenty minutes, or more if one has time for further reflection on the readings.

The two "hinge" (principal) hours, Morning Prayer and Evening Prayer, follow essentially the same pattern. After an invocation of God's help and a brief prayer of praise, the hour begins with a hymn. As a hymn, ideally this is sung, though in individual prayer it is often recited. Two psalms and a biblical canticle follow, each introduced and concluded by an antiphon. A short passage from Scripture is next read, together with a prayer of response to its message. A Gospel canticle—Zechariah's Benedictus in the morning and Mary's Magnificat in the evening—with its antiphon is then prayed. The hour concludes with intercessions for various needs, the Our Father, and a final prayer.

Daytime Prayer consists of a hymn, three psalms, a short scriptural reading, and a final prayer. Night Prayer follows a similar pattern, shortened, however, to one psalm and with prayers appropriate to the day's end. The Office of Readings begins with a hymn and three psalms that prepare for two longer readings, one from the Bible and the other from a Church Father, a saint, or another classic spiritual writer. These readings offer daily nourishment for reflection and meditation.

The Liturgy of the Hours harmonizes with the Mass of the day. If, for example, the Mass is for the Second Sunday of Advent, then Morning Prayer, the Office of Readings, and the other hours will focus on the theme of Advent: preparing for the coming of Jesus. If the Mass of the day is the memorial of Saint Thérèse, the Liturgy of the Hours will also center on her life and message. In this way, the Liturgy of the Hours prolongs the grace of the Mass throughout the day.

Monks pray the entire Liturgy of the Hours in their monastic churches, gathering at regular intervals during the day and night. Active religious pray parts of it together each day in their chapels or churches. Parish priests pray the entire Liturgy of the Hours daily in their rectories or churches, most often as individual prayer. Deacons pray some or all of the Hours during the day, again most often individually.

Laypersons pray the Liturgy of the Hours in varied ways. In some parishes, Morning Prayer is said before or after Mass, and all are invited. In other settings, like the university church already mentioned, laypeople also gather for the Liturgy of the Hours. Often laypersons pray individually those parts of the Liturgy of the Hours compatible with their occupations of family and work. They may pray Morning Prayer before the day's tasks or in church after daily Mass. They may pray it on their tablet or smartphone as they ride the commuter train or subway. They may listen to the Office of Readings or Evening Prayer in the car driving to work or to school to meet the children. The Liturgy of the Hours may be prayed in many settings; in each, it will bless the day.

Most deeply, the Liturgy of the Hours is our sharing in "the hymn of praise that is sung through all the ages in the heavenly places."[20] When the members of a closely united family gather, each delights in the love, goodness, and talents of the others and finds suitable ways to express that delight. In the Triune God, this delight in the Others is experienced to an infinite degree. With a gladness that knows no bounds, each rejoices in the love, goodness, wisdom, and self-giving of the Others. From this mutual joy is born a "hymn of praise" that is "sung through all the ages" in the eternal communion of the Trinity.

When one of these Persons became man, for the first time that eternal hymn of praise was sung *in this world* by a human heart and on human lips. Jesus, the Word made flesh, willed that his people join in that hymn of praise. Our praying of the Liturgy of the Hours, the Church tells us, is a sharing in that eternal hymn of praise.[21] "We do not know how to pray as we ought," Saint Paul writes, but "the Spirit helps us in our weakness" and "himself intercedes for us with sighs too deep for words" (Rom 8:26).[22] The Spirit takes our weak, limited prayer and lifts it to Jesus, our Mediator with the Father. Jesus unites this prayer with his own, enriching it beyond all measure in power, efficacy, and beauty, and so presents it to his Father. This, the Church affirms, occurs every time we pray the Liturgy of the Hours; this is the root of its unique dignity as prayer and the source of its power in our lives.

Such is the Liturgy of the Hours. This book shares one person's experience of it through forty years.

Chapter 1

Beginnings

*When you come to the Office . . . it
is as if you were dropping in on a
conversation already in progress—
a conversation between God and men
which began long before you were born.*
—From Evensong, Coventry Cathedral

I FIRST ENCOUNTERED the Liturgy of the Hours through
my pastor, Father James Wolfe. For twenty-seven years, the
years in which I grew up, he was pastor of Most Holy Rosary
parish in the town of Maine, New York. When he arrived,
there was no Catholic church. The former town inn served
as a temporary church, and Father Wolfe lived upstairs in
the space that later became the choir loft. His task was to
create an independent parish from what had been a mission
of a parish in nearby Binghamton, New York. He fulfilled
that goal, building a rectory and church and establishing the
full range of parochial life: Masses, confessions, catechism,
baptisms, weddings, and the rest.

I came to know Most Holy Rosary well, first as an altar
boy and later, in high school, through young adult activities. Looking back, I recognize that Father Wolfe saw in me
a vocation to the priesthood and created an environment in
which this call could grow. He gave me spiritual books to
read that gradually deepened my understanding of the faith,
and he asked me to help in parish activities. As I shared the

life of the parish, read about the faith, and worked with
him, priesthood as a way of life grew familiar.

When the time came, and I knew that I wished to pursue
this calling, I spoke with Father Wolfe. He guided my discernment and, when I had made my choice, accompanied
me to the seminary. I will be forever grateful to him.

One image of Father Wolfe remains indelibly fixed in
my memory. The following scenario repeated a number of
times. I would arrive at the rectory to help him with a parish activity. I would ring the doorbell, he would answer,
and I would enter the large front room that was the parish
office. Then he would ask that I wait a few minutes while
he finished praying the Liturgy of the Hours. This is the
image I still see: I am seated in that office, looking through
whatever reading material was at hand—a parish bulletin,
a life of a saint, a volume of Church history—very aware of
Father Wolfe across the room, seated at his desk, breviary in
hand, silently praying. After some minutes, he would close
the book, rise, and we would proceed to the activity at hand.

We never spoke about the Liturgy of the Hours. It certainly never occurred to me that I might pray it. But that
was my introduction to this prayer: the witness of a parish
priest faithfully committed to it, choosing to find time each
day, in the midst of his activity, to say the Hours. The image
of his fidelity to the Liturgy of the Hours stayed with me
and shaped my earliest impression of it.

I JOINED MY RELIGIOUS COMMUNITY, the Oblates of the
Virgin Mary, in 1972, and I began my studies toward religious vows and priesthood. At that time, this training took
place in Rome, Italy. We studied at the pontifical universi-
ties and received spiritual formation in our own residence.

I did not know it then, but I had entered the seminary
just as the renewed Liturgy of the Hours was introduced in
the Church. At this point, the renewal of the Divine Office

mandated by the Second Vatican Council was complete. In 1971, one year before I entered, the new Liturgy of the Hours was promulgated, and publication of the Latin edition began. The last of the Latin volumes appeared in 1972, just as I commenced my studies toward priesthood. The translation of these volumes into modern languages would require more time. The final volume of the English translation was published four years later, in 1976. I entered the seminary, therefore, in an "in-between" phase, when the older Divine Office was no longer in use and the new Liturgy of the Hours was not yet available in English.

In my first two years of seminary, we prayed the only English version of the Divine Office available to us: the Latin-English edition published in 1963.[1] Because the new Liturgy of the Hours had already been approved, it was not liturgically correct to use this earlier Office. The transition had barely begun, however, and we were in Italy, with no other English text at hand.

I have always been thankful that I had a taste, at least, of the earlier Divine Office. During those two years, we prayed Morning Prayer, Evening Prayer, and Night Prayer—Lauds, Vespers, and Compline, as these were titled in the former Office. My clearest memory is of the length of that preconciliar Office with respect to the new Liturgy of the Hours. Both Lauds and Vespers had five psalms; Morning and Evening Prayer in the new Liturgy of the Hours have three. Compline in the earlier Office had three psalms; the new Night Prayer, either one or two. In subsequent years, if recitation of the Liturgy of the Hours seemed long, I would remember that former Office, grateful for the renewal mandated by Vatican II.

When I began praying the Office, I found myself confronted with volumes of two thousand to three thousand pages, with six ribbons to place in their proper pages for the hour of prayer. My companions and I gradually learned how to find the psalms for the day, how to pray the Office for the liturgical seasons (Advent, Christmas, Lent, and Easter), which texts to pray for a particular feast day or saint, and so forth. Because we prayed the Office in common, we had guidance in this process, and this greatly eased these initial difficulties.[2] As time passed, we grew more familiar with the rubrics of the Office. Generally, we could find the right pages, though on more complicated days we might again need assistance.

DURING MY SECOND YEAR of seminary, Pope Paul VI published his apostolic exhortation *Marialis Cultus*. This document discussed devotion to Mary in the postconciliar Church, and I read it with interest. In the final section, the pope recalled the Council's description of the family as a "domestic church" and the importance of prayer together as a family.[3] He cited the recommendation in the *General Instruction of the Liturgy of the Hours*—the text in which the Church explains the nature and practice of this prayer—regarding the family and the Liturgy of the Hours: "It is desirable that the family, the domestic sanctuary of the Church, should not only pray together to God but should also celebrate some parts of the Liturgy of the Hours as occasion offers, so as to enter more deeply into the life of the Church."[4] The pope added, "No avenue should be left unexplored to ensure that this clear and practical recommendation finds within Christian families growing and joyful acceptance," and he described the Liturgy of the Hours as "the high point which family prayer can reach."[5] After the Liturgy of the Hours, he said, the rosary "should be considered as one of the best and most efficacious prayers in common that the Christian family is invited to recite."[6]

I read these words with interior resistance. The family rosary was familiar. We had prayed it in my home, and I knew of other families that did so as well. I had never heard, however, of any family that prayed the Liturgy of the Hours. Though I never voiced my thoughts, in my heart I doubted this was possible. Still, I never forgot the pope's words. They questioned my understanding of family prayer—the Liturgy of the Hours, the pope taught, was its *high* point—and I did not know how to harmonize his words with my own sense of family prayer. Only decades later would I see that the family can indeed pray parts of the Liturgy of the Hours and that such prayer greatly blesses it.

AFTER OUR FIRST TWO YEARS of seminary, my companions and I entered the novitiate. This was a year without university studies, dedicated totally to formation in the spiritual life. Under the guidance of our novice master, a wise and experienced Oblate priest, we learned about prayer, our religious vows, the life of our founder, the Venerable Bruno Lanteri, and the mission he gave to us in the Church.

During our novitiate, we began using the new Liturgy of the Hours. We prayed it from a single volume that included Morning Prayer, Evening Prayer, and Night Prayer. Every morning, after a time of personal meditation, we gathered in the chapel for Morning Prayer and Mass. During a holy hour before supper, we said Evening Prayer together. At 9:00 P.M., we prayed Night Prayer.

I lived this experience of the Liturgy of the Hours a second time when, after ordination, I was assigned as an assistant to the same novice master. I remember with fondness the Night Prayer that ended the day. Our novitiate had just moved into a retreat house in Rome, newly acquired by our superiors for this purpose. The chapel was small, and when we gathered for prayer, we sat crowded on folding chairs that overflowed into the room beyond. In its own way, even the limited space united us as night fell. There, in the warm, yellow-tinged light of the chapel, surrounded by darkness, we prayed Night Prayer. One novice that year was a skilled organist, and he made Night Prayer musically beautiful. To his accompaniment, we concluded the prayer by singing the Salve Regina or another classic Marian antiphon.[7] Then we entered the silence that would continue until Mass the next morning. It was an uplifting conclusion to the day, and it prepared us for the night to follow.

During my novitiate, I prayed the Liturgy of the Hours with goodwill: it was part of a program I accepted and from which I wished to learn. Praying Morning Prayer, Evening Prayer, and Night Prayer together every day for a year taught us much about the Liturgy of the Hours. We grew familiar with its many aspects, found increasing ease in its recitation, and embraced it as an unquestioned part of the day. By the end of novitiate, the daily Liturgy of the Hours was an accepted part of life.

AFTER OUR NOVITIATE, we resumed classes. For the next four years, we pursued the theological studies that prepared us for ordination. We lived in a residence attached to an Oblate parish just outside the walls of Rome. From there, we commuted daily to the university.

When we began these studies, we received the four-volume set of the Liturgy of the Hours published that same year, 1975.[8] During those four years, we continued the practice of our novitiate, praying Morning Prayer, Evening Prayer, and Night Prayer together, now, however, in the more active context of studies and preparation for ministry. Night Prayer, in particular, we found difficult to schedule, since the priests and seminarians divided for various activities after supper. We prayed it at the table at the end of supper, an arrangement that allowed us to pray it together, but that sat uneasily with the meaning of Night Prayer, intended to close the day.

We prayed the Liturgy of the Hours daily throughout those years, and the habits established in our novitiate grew more rooted. I cannot remember if I also read the *General Instruction of the Liturgy of the Hours*—the seventy-seven-page text in which the Church explains the theology and practice of this prayer and the key document, therefore, for understanding the Liturgy of the Hours.[9] If I did, it was only in part and rapidly, so that I retained little. My failure to assimilate this text would cause many struggles in the years to come.

I decided that I would read at least one book on the Liturgy of the Hours. I chose a concise introduction written by Father Vincenzo Raffa, a central figure in the renewal of the Liturgy of the Hours.[10] I liked his writing. He was a master of his subject and wrote succinctly, clearly, and with depth. He helped me understand the Liturgy of the Hours as *the prayer of the Church*. When I prayed the psalms, for example, with their varied sentiments of joy, anguish, praise, and supplication, I knew that I gave voice to the prayer of the whole Church: those whose hearts that day were filled with joy or burdened by sorrow, who lifted their hearts in praise or cried out their need to God. Father Raffa's book was my principal source for understanding the Liturgy of the Hours, and for years, I kept it on my shelf.

This decision to read one book on the Liturgy of the Hours was helpful but also included a limitation. My thinking at the time might be expressed as follows: "Now I have read a good introduction to the Liturgy of the Hours. I now possess the understanding I need to pray it. Further exploration of its meaning and spirituality may be helpful but is not really necessary. I am now prepared to pray the Liturgy of the Hours for the rest of my life." Almost forty years would pass before I grasped the limitations of my understanding and how these impacted my prayer of the Liturgy of the Hours.

ONE KEY COMPONENT of those four years of studies was sacred Scripture. We took classes on both the Old and New Testaments: the historical books, wisdom literature, and prophets of the Old Testament and the synoptic Gospels (Matthew, Mark, and Luke), the Acts of the Apostles with the letters of Saint Paul, and the Johannine writings (Gospel of John, three Letters, and Revelation) of the New Testament.

For two of these courses, we had the same professor. He taught the wisdom books of the Old Testament—Job, Psalms, Proverbs, Ecclesiastes, the Song of Solomon, and the rest—and the Johannine writings in the New Testament. His style was dry, but his content was rich and repaid the effort to listen. He is a teacher I remember with lasting gratitude. His courses, in a special way, opened for me the Scriptures and showed me how to study them. In particular, his presentation of the Gospel of John, an exploration of its twenty-one chapters verse by verse, revealed to me new and inspiring depths in the Bible.

One decision he made, however, deeply affected my praying of the Liturgy of the Hours. When he taught us the wisdom books, he explained that time did not allow a full treatment of each book and that some selection was necessary. In the Liturgy of the Hours, he said, we would spend a lifetime gaining familiarity with the Psalms, but we would have less contact with the remaining books: Ecclesiastes, Sirach, Wisdom, and the others. He thought it best, therefore, to omit the Psalms in his course and dedicate more time to the other books.

This choice certainly permitted deeper exploration of these wisdom books, but it also signified that I completed my years of theology without having studied the Psalms. Because I was praying the psalms every day, year after year, they did indeed become familiar. I could recite the words with ease: "The Lord is my light and my help; whom shall I fear?" (Ps 27); "O purify me, then I shall be clean; O wash me, I shall be whiter than snow" (Ps 51); "How lovely is your dwelling place, Lord, God of hosts" (Ps 84); "Cry out with joy to the Lord, all the earth. Serve the Lord with gladness" (Ps 100).[11] These and many other lines from the psalms became part of my spiritual vocabulary.

I did not see, however, that familiarity may not equal understanding. When, for example, were the psalms written? By whom? Was there meaning in the structure of the book of Psalms—the sequence of these one hundred and fifty prayers? What did it mean for a Christian to pray Jewish prayers? How did the individual psalms relate to Christ? It is striking to me now that I could pray the psalms for so many years and never consider these questions. Had these questions been put to me, my answers would have been superficial at best.

Year after year, too, I read words in the psalms that I did not understand: "You crushed the monster Rahab and killed it" (Ps 89); "I will triumph and divide the land of Shechem; I will measure out the valley of Succoth" (Ps 108); "Alas, that I abide a stranger in Meshech, dwell among the tents of Kedar!" (Ps 120); and other verses like these.[12] A commentary would have explained these lines, but I never thought of reading one. As the years passed, therefore, I prayed such verses with familiarity but without understanding.

My failure to pursue a deeper grasp of the psalms did not arise from bad will; I simply did not recognize the need. Yet goodwill and daily contact could not substitute for lack of understanding. That limitation, too, would impact my praying of the Liturgy of the Hours for years to come.

MY THIRD YEAR of theology ended, and ordination to the diaconate was now only months away. With the diaconate would come the commitment to pray the full Liturgy of the Hours daily for the rest of my life. I remember the evening before ordination and my awareness that, beginning the next day, a new seriousness would enter my prayer of the Liturgy of the Hours. Now I would pray it by mandate of the Church and would be held to pray it daily, in its entirety.

A sense of the significance of this step and of commitment to this prayer marked my day of diaconal ordination.

There was nothing dramatic about this. I had long known that the Church requires this promise of deacons and priests, and I accepted it. During the ceremony, the bishop asks the candidate, "Are you resolved to maintain and deepen a spirit of prayer appropriate to your way of life and, in keeping with what is required of you, to celebrate faithfully the Liturgy of the Hours for the Church and for the whole world?" The candidate replies, "I am."[13] I gave that answer fully intending to be faithful to this promise.

All in the Church are warmly invited to pray the Liturgy of the Hours. Some, by mandate of the Church, promise to pray it and are canonically bound to this promise. Priests and deacons to be ordained as priests promise to pray the entire Liturgy of the Hours daily; permanent deacons promise to pray those Hours prescribed by their conference of bishops; religious men and women commit to all or part of it according to their constitutions.[14] Now, decades after ordination, I believe that when the canonical duty to pray the Liturgy of the Hours exists, the decision to be faithful to that duty determines everything else regarding the Liturgy of the Hours—whether this prayer will mature and deepen over the years, or whether it will languish and remain marginal in life.

I do not believe that mere fidelity to an obligation is enough. I do believe, however, that without this faithful commitment to the promise taken, the "more" that comes only with prolonged praying of the Liturgy of the Hours will not be experienced.

I took that promise seriously. Many times it was the one thing that kept me praying the Liturgy of the Hours, and I am grateful for it.

Nonetheless, I viewed the Liturgy of the Hours as something complementary in my life of prayer, something that came after what I thought more important. If asked, I would have readily agreed that liturgical prayer, as the Church's official prayer, is primary in the spiritual life. I understood that the Mass is the center of all Christian prayer. Knowing, too, that the Liturgy of the Hours is liturgical prayer, I acknowledged its key role in my life of prayer. But for me, in practice, the true center was my time of meditation on Scripture.

Several factors shaped this conviction. Before entering the seminary, I had learned from Saint Francis de Sales's *Introduction to the Devout Life* the value of such meditation. From the conferences of Archbishop Fulton Sheen, I absorbed the importance of daily prayer before the Blessed Sacrament in a priest's life. In the writings of Venerable Bruno Lanteri, the founder of my community, I encountered a similar insistence. We were to begin the day, he taught, with meditation. If we could not because of ministerial obligations, we were to dedicate the first free moment to this meditation. If no single time was available, we were to find two shorter times. The Venerable Lanteri evidently held such meditation in high esteem and desired that his spiritual sons do likewise.

We began daily meditation as novices, dedicating an hour to this before Morning Prayer and Mass. We continued this practice during our theological studies with a daily hour of prayer before the Blessed Sacrament. Shortly before my ordination as deacon, I made the thirty-day Ignatian Spiritual Exercises and was taught again and more deeply how to meditate.

I saw no contradiction between personal meditation on Scripture and the Church's liturgical prayer. I understood the Church's vision of these as complementary. Yet if the decision to pray the Liturgy of the Hours was fundamental, I thought it clear that the decision to meditate daily on Scripture was more fundamental still. The quality of my liturgical prayer, I believed, depended on my personal meditation. Having encountered Jesus in meditation on his Word, I would be ready for fruitful liturgical prayer. In this sense, the truly key decision in my life of prayer seemed the decision to pray daily with Scripture.

I did not know how to resolve this divergence—my theoretical acceptance of liturgical prayer as primary and, at the same time, my practical view of personal meditation as the key prayer. This was not a major concern, however, and it did not impede my daily life of prayer. Still, I occasionally wondered about this discrepancy and what it said about my prayer.

As ORDINATION TO PRIESTHOOD NEARED, my parents asked what I wished for an ordination gift. They expected, I think, that I would ask for a chalice and were surprised when I asked instead for the four volumes of the Liturgy of the Hours in Latin. I still have that set of Latin volumes with the handwritten inscription, "On the joyful occasion of your Ordination to the Sacred Priesthood, with love, Mother and Dad." I used it frequently in my first years of priesthood and occasionally in subsequent years.

My interest in the Latin version did not arise from a desire to pray the Hours in the original language—to pray, for example, Saint Ambrose's hymns or to read Saint Augustine's sermons as they wrote them. That was a nice bonus. The primary reason for my interest was my need to improve my Latin.

The year before ordination, I had begun graduate studies in spiritual theology. From the time I entered my community, I had been drawn to its founder, the Venerable Bruno Lanteri, and I planned to write my thesis on his spirituality. Because he wrote in Latin, I needed to read it well for my thesis. I had studied Latin in earlier years; the Liturgy of the Hours would provide daily exercise in reading it—and since the Hours were already part of my day, it would do so without requiring additional time. Praying the Hours in Latin might be slower than in English, but greater ease in reading Latin would amply compensate for that.

I knew that I would not understand the Latin as well as the English. Nonetheless, my desire to learn this language, the richness of the original text, and my expectation that, with practice, my comprehension would improve led me to accept this limitation. I realized that in part, at least, I was "using" the Liturgy of the Hours for a purpose other than prayer, and at times I felt some disquiet about this. Yet I continued to pray the Hours in Latin.

Four years after ordination, I was assigned to work with our seminarians in pretheological studies. When we needed a teacher for Latin, I volunteered. I wanted to meet a need in the community, but I also knew that teaching Latin would improve my command of it. During the years that I taught this course, I prayed the Liturgy of the Hours in Latin. This was valuable "practice" and helped me in my teaching. Once more, the Liturgy of the Hours served an academic purpose.

Reviewing my first years of priesthood, I can summarize my approach to the Liturgy of the Hours in the following way. My commitment to it was sincere, and I fully intended to maintain it. I had a certain but limited understanding of its theological meaning. The Psalms were growing familiar through repetition, but I had never studied them, and my knowledge of them was incomplete.

In those years, the Liturgy of the Hours was an established part of my life. I thought myself prepared to pray it and never imagined that I had more to learn. The Hours were both prayer and a means toward academic goals. And for me, personal meditation was more fundamental; the Hours were its complement, helping me to pray the rest of the day. This combination of sincere commitment and limited understanding left me vulnerable to the struggles that would follow.

Chapter 2

Questions

The only force I believe in is prayer, and it is a force I apply with more doggedness than attention.
—Flannery O'Connor

For twelve years after ordination, apart from a year in a parish, I worked with our seminarians. I continued, therefore, to pray the Liturgy of the Hours in a seminary residence and with seminarians. Our Oblate constitutions urge us to pray Morning Prayer, Evening Prayer, and Night Prayer in common, and in the ordered life of a seminary, this was not difficult. The Office of Readings and Midday Prayer I said on my own.

During these years, my interest in Ignatian prayer grew. I learned Saint Ignatius's teaching on the meditation and contemplation of Scripture. I explored his examen prayer and the rules for discernment that underlie it. Later I wrote books on these topics and taught them in retreats and seminars. I welcomed the new understanding this research brought me and sensed how this deeper insight blessed my prayer. Saint Ignatius's guidance on how to prepare for prayer, how to begin it, how to engage the mind and the imagination, how to note attractions and resistances in prayer, and how to perceive their significance, greatly assisted me. His counsel offered fresh insight into prayer with Scripture, and I was grateful for it.

But I never thought of studying the Liturgy of the Hours in a similar way. As the years passed, my prayer of the Hours remained what it had been at ordination: I prayed it with the same understanding received as a seminarian. In retrospect, I marvel that I felt no need to learn more about a prayer that occupied *over an hour of every day.*

While working with the seminarians, I taught a course on the Second Vatican Council. I have before me as I write the battered copy of the Council's documents I used, underlined and annotated throughout. I welcomed the opportunity to learn the Council's teachings more deeply. During the course, I taught the chapter of the Constitution on the Sacred Liturgy dedicated to the Divine Office. In a few paragraphs, the Council offered a rich theology of the Liturgy of the Hours. There I read of "that hymn which is sung throughout all ages in the halls of heaven" and how Jesus, taking human flesh, introduced this hymn into our world. I learned and taught my students that in the Liturgy of the Hours, Jesus associates us with that eternal hymn and that "by celebrating the Eucharist and by other means, especially the celebration of the Divine Office," the Church "is ceaselessly engaged in praising the Lord and interceding for the salvation of the world."[1] In my copy of the documents, each of the lines quoted is underlined in the now faded red ink I used as I prepared my classes.

I studied the Council's words, assimilated them, and presented them to the students. Yet my prayer of the Hours remained unchanged. The course on Vatican II was one of several I was teaching, each requiring preparation. And in that course, these were only a few paragraphs in a large document, itself one of sixteen to be taught. For a moment, therefore, I focused on the meaning of the Liturgy of the Hours, but that moment was lost in the press of many activities and had no further resonance.

Something similar occurred three years later when I was named novice master. I adopted with the novices the practice of my own novitiate: we prayed Morning Prayer, Evening Prayer, and Night Prayer together. I prepared the year by selecting texts on prayer, religious life, and other spiritual topics to explore together. Among these was an introduction to the Liturgy of the Hours. We covered many of these texts that year, but not this last. I thought then that this was due to lack of time—that there was too much to teach in one year. Now I am less sure: How could I have taught the Liturgy of the Hours well when I knew so little of it myself? How could I have prepared the novices to pray it throughout their lives when my own understanding of it was so limited? I suspect now that I avoided the text on the Liturgy of the Hours because, on some level, I knew that I was not qualified to teach it.

IN THOSE FIRST YEARS OF PRIESTHOOD, I heard two remarks about the Liturgy of the Hours that stayed in my memory. One was said by a Carmelite priest whom we invited to our community to give a day of retreat. In his conference, he told of a priest who finished reciting the Office and said, "Now that I've completed the Office, I can pray!" The Carmelite rhetorically asked the priest, "And what were you just doing?" I was struck by this question, because frequently I would feel like that priest: having "gotten through" the hymns, psalms, readings, and invocations of the Liturgy of the Hours, I would finally feel free to pray—free to follow my heart without the confinement of prescribed prayers. From time to time, I thought of this anecdote with a twinge of uneasiness: perhaps all was not well with my prayer of the Liturgy of the Hours.

Later, a Dominican came to speak to our seminarians. He compared Morning Prayer in the Liturgy of the Hours to "our morning cornflakes." If we wrote a letter to another, he said, we would never think to mention that we had cornflakes for breakfast, but if we did not have them, we would miss the nourishment they give. Similarly, he said, the Liturgy of the Hours is a "routine" part of the day; yet in its absence, we would miss the spiritual nourishment it provides.

At the time, I found myself nodding agreement. That metaphor described my own sense of the Liturgy of the Hours. I prayed it daily and would have felt something missing without it. But I was not excited about it. The Liturgy of the Hours was a staple, my "morning cornflakes," an "ordinary" part of each day and no more.

AFTER FOUR YEARS of priesthood in Italy, my superior sent me to Boston to help with our seminarians. Shortly after I arrived, I was asked to say a weekly Mass in Spanish. Our community staffed a chapel in Boston that offered, among other services, a Sunday Mass for the local Hispanic community. I had never celebrated Mass in Spanish and welcomed the challenge. For the next five years, I was intensely engaged in Hispanic ministry. Needing to learn the language and culture, I made several trips to Latin America. I enjoyed my time in the Dominican Republic, Argentina, and Chile and especially the many people I came to know. I returned from these trips with nostalgia for the persons, places, and experiences I had encountered.

Early in this ministry, I acquired a one-volume breviary in Spanish. Again with Spanish, as before with Latin, the Liturgy of the Hours helped me learn a language. On Sundays I would say Morning Prayer aloud in Spanish as a vocal "warm-up" for the Spanish Mass. As with Latin, I focused more on the language than on the content of the psalms and prayers. The Spanish Liturgy of the Hours also awakened memories of Latin America: holding the same book I had used there, reading its pages, and saying the prayers in Spanish, I could see again the places and people with whom I had prayed it in those countries. During those five years, I often prayed the Liturgy of the Hours in Spanish.

In 1991, I was named provincial for the United States Province of my religious community. I exercised that role for the next ten years. Every year, the provincials from around the world met with our general government to review our congregation's life. Each time, we gathered in a different country.

One year, we met in Rome. We stayed in our General House on the Janiculum Hill, not far from Saint Peter's, above the Trastevere section of Rome. We would meet all morning, break for lunch (and siesta), and resume our meeting until supper at 8:00 P.M. After supper, a group of us would walk down the hill to the Basilica of Santa Maria in Trastevere. There the community of Sant'Egidio, dedicated laymen and laywomen, gathered for Evening Prayer from the Liturgy of the Hours. I grew to love those visits to the basilica. The beauty of the church, the prayerfulness of the community, the singing of the psalms, and the heart-felt homilies on Scripture all created a welcome sense of prayer after a day of meetings. Still today I remember some of those homilies.

The prayer of these men and women inspired me, and I purchased a copy of the book they used for Morning and Evening Prayer. I especially liked the introduction to each psalm provided in the book, and for a time, I used it in my own prayer. I did not realize it then, but these brief introductions were my first formation in the Psalms. I liked them because, having read them, I understood the psalm better and so could pray it more deeply. I used the book for several months after I returned from Rome but did not persevere in this practice.

Meeting in a different country each year meant encountering a different language each time. The need to learn these languages for research and for communication within the congregation led me to repeat what I had done with Latin and Spanish. Each year, I would purchase a one-volume breviary in that language. I would use it before the trip, during the meetings, and for some months after. As before, I focused more on learning the language than on the prayers themselves. I was aware of this and, once more, a little troubled by it, but it did not stop me.

A parallel situation occurred when, years later, I underwent vocal surgery. The recovery included several months of voice therapy with daily vocal exercises. The Liturgy of the Hours was the "perfect" way to build these exercises into the day without taking time from other activities. I recited the Hours out loud in my room, attentive to correct posture, breathing, and vocal placement. The Liturgy of the Hours again helped me acquire a skill, and here, too, I attended more to the skill than to the prayers. As before, I felt some misgivings but continued this practice.

WHEN I COMPLETED MY YEARS as provincial, I was given a time of sabbatical. I chose to spend it in a parish, exercising daily ministry but with limited responsibilities. This proved an ideal mixture of activity and time to replenish my energies. The pastor had just lost his assistant and was pleased to have a second priest in the parish.

He explained that he and the former assistant had prayed Morning Prayer at 7:00 A.M. in the rectory chapel. I willingly agreed to continue the practice. We did this several times a week for a number of months, though eventually it grew less consistent. I always liked this time together in the morning. The chapel was open to parishioners, but at that hour, only the two of us were present. We said Morning Prayer as given in the breviary, without singing, extra invocations, or the like. When we had finished, we often sat and talked for a while. The pastor would tell me of the day's activities and might ask if I could say a Mass, help with a funeral, and so on. Morning Prayer offered an opportunity to communicate as the day began, and I welcomed it. When this practice became less frequent, I missed it.

After my sabbatical, I began an active ministry of retreats and seminars. For the first eight months of the year, I traveled for these engagements; the final months I dedicated to writing. I loved both the speaking and the writing.

Many of the retreats and seminars required such intense labor that I could not pray the Liturgy of the Hours during them. I knew the Church did not require me to pray it in such circumstances and was at peace with this.[2]

Other retreats and seminars, however, left some time for personal prayer, and then I was less sure. Preparing for and giving conferences required concentrated mental effort. During these retreats—somewhat unwisely—I also continued my reading toward whatever book I was writing. When I turned to prayer, I had little energy for reflection on the psalms, readings, and other elements of the Hours. I preferred a personal prayer in which I could simply be with the Lord and follow my heart's leading. When I prayed during these retreats, I did so in this unstructured manner.

I often wondered whether I should pray at least part of the Liturgy of the Hours during these retreats. At times, I would be one of a team of directors and would see others pray the Liturgy of the Hours during the retreat. I remember in particular one priest with whom I shared many retreats. Every time, I would see him pray the Liturgy of the Hours. When I did, the question of my own practice would trouble me anew. Once I discussed this with an older priest who had spent his life giving retreats. He told me that these struggles are part of the ministry of retreats, that we never find a perfect balance, and that I should not worry about this. His counsel helped, and I often recalled it.

I recognize now that in these retreats I generally attempted too much with too little help. Often I would be alone to give several conferences a day, meet with individual retreatants, and guide the times of group prayer. I would rise early to prepare my conferences and homilies and would not stop until late in the evening. Consequently, I was simply too worn to pray the Liturgy of the Hours. After many years, I learned to moderate the work and to give retreats with a team. Then praying the Liturgy of the Hours became more possible.

But intense labor was not the only reason I shied away from the Liturgy of the Hours.

DURING THESE YEARS, I often rebelled interiorly against the Liturgy of the Hours. I do not wish to exaggerate this. I never stopped praying the Liturgy of the Hours, and my commitment to it never wavered. I also knew that it helped me spiritually and apostolically in various ways. But I did not want to spend any extra time on it. My personal meditation was my unhurried time of prayer. I said the Liturgy of the Hours, but I kept the recitation moving and was impatient with anything that lengthened it.

I felt this resistance when tired or spiritually desolate.[3] At such times, I had little desire to pray, and the Liturgy of the Hours was something to "get done." I also felt it in times when I sincerely wanted to pray. Then the "morning cornflakes" and "daily faithfulness" understanding of the Liturgy of the Hours was insufficient. It was too little; it was not the prayer of the heart that I desired.

This resistance arose on another level as well. In my twenty-fifth year of priesthood, I wrote in my journal: "The reason why the Liturgy of the Hours is not attractive is because I'm always taking in so much content that this just feels like more, and it is content that I have not chosen." I had experienced this as provincial and felt it again in my years of public speaking and writing. The days were filled with content: hours of reading, prolonged reflection, painstaking efforts to write well, undivided attention to others in meetings, and so forth. When I approached the Liturgy of the Hours, its psalms and prayers simply felt like "more content" to assimilate when I had already absorbed so much. And while I could choose my own reading according to my interest, in the Liturgy of the Hours, someone else, with different tastes, had chosen it for me.

My practice of the Liturgy of the Hours accorded with these sentiments. On Sundays and solemnities, when we gathered in community to pray the Hours, we would sing rather than recite the hymns and psalms. I never liked this: it took too long, I was not a monk, the pace was too slow, and so forth. When I gave retreats to contemplative nuns, I admired their dedication to the Liturgy of the Hours. I watched them gather five and more times a day to sing it. But I never felt personally called to this. In one retreat, a loudspeaker carried the chanting of the Hours into my room. The sisters apologized and told me they could not shut it off in my room without also shutting it off in the rooms of the elderly and infirm sisters who participated in this way. For a week, I lived with the singing of the Hours five times a day, confirmed in my conviction that this was not my vocation.

At one point, our superior introduced pauses between the psalms and a longer pause after the scriptural reading. I resented this and, during the longer pauses, would pray part of another Hour for that day. In personal recitation, I looked for the shortest invitatory psalm and for the shortest hymn among the choices provided. I rarely prayed the optional psalm prayers, never prayed the optional verses of the Te Deum, and never added the optional hours for Midday Prayer. When I learned that in private recitation I need not pray the antiphons that divide a psalm into parts, I was pleased, not because—as the Church intends—the psalm thus flows in its unbroken integrity and so fosters devotion, but because the Hour would be a little shorter.[4] I would say the opening verses of an Hour while setting the ribbons and the first lines of the Te Deum while turning to its page. It was a faithful recitation of the Liturgy of the Hours, and in some ways it was fruitful, but always it was a prayer to be said and completed.

Yet I wanted to pray the Liturgy of the Hours well and tried repeatedly to attain this end. On one retreat, I walked every morning to the lake on the retreat grounds. I would sit on the shore as the sun rose and the fog lifted from the water. There, in the quiet of the early hours, I would say Morning Prayer and the Office of Reading. I prayed some of the words out loud and found that this helped me grasp their meaning. I recalled that the Psalms are songs intended to be prayed and sung aloud. I resolved that in praying the Hours I would say occasional lines of the psalms out loud. After the retreat, I did this for a time. On another occasion, I decided to say one line of each verse out loud. I found that this did not slow the prayer significantly and that it, too, helped me pray the psalm with attention. This practice also I continued for some months.

But none of these efforts lasted. Each awakened the hope that "Now I have found the key." My inability to sustain them, however, always led to disappointment. With resignation, I would return to my habitual recitation of the Hours.

One community of sisters to which I gave retreats prayed the Office of Readings in common. Each time, I gave a retreat, I joined them for this prayer. After the psalms, a sister would proclaim the scriptural and patristic readings out loud while the community listened. I found the spoken proclamation helpful. A homily, for example, of Saint Augustine or Saint John Chrysostom would gain new life when spoken aloud. I tried to do the same when praying the Office of Readings on my own, but this, like my other attempts, did not last.

One fall, I was a guest at a college for several months of writing. During that time, I prayed the Liturgy of the Hours entirely on my own. In this setting, too, I sought ways to say the Hours more prayerfully. It occurred to me that I could find the hymn on the Internet—this was before electronic versions of the Hours were available—play it softly, and join in the singing. I did this and liked it. Yet the search could take some time, and I could not always find the hymn I sought. After a few weeks, I abandoned this practice.

On another occasion, I tried praying systematically through the hymns provided for Midday Prayer and Night Prayer. Each day, I chose a different hymn from the selection offered, praying through them in sequence. I found this helpful and repeated this two or three times. Yet another time, I focused on the psalm titles and the introductory sentence for each psalm. In one retreat, still unsure of whether or not to pray the Hours, I tried a compromise: I prayed one psalm from each of the Hours.

Still later, I changed the readings of the Office of Readings. I grew weary of repeating the same readings year after year and sought new material from other classic spiritual texts. I knew that in some countries, the bishops provided a wider choice of readings, and I wanted something similar.[5] I took matters into my own hands. One day I was on a plane with another of our priests, traveling home from meetings. As we flew, I began praying the Office of Readings. When I finished the psalms, I brought out my New Testament and read the next segment of the letter of Saint Paul I had chosen. Then I opened my copy of Saint Teresa of Avila's *The Way of Perfection* and read the next few pages. Seated beside me, my fellow priest noticed, understood what I was doing, and commented on my choice of readings. I felt a little sheepish but continued this practice, too, for a time.

I was trying. I was using every means I knew to render the Liturgy of the Hours more prayerful. Periodically, I renewed these efforts or variations of them. I liked them, and they helped. Yet none lasted, and none significantly changed my prayer of the Hours.

I did not understand that I needed to go *deeper* into the Liturgy of the Hours. As a result, all I could do was try *harder*. I could begin these efforts, but I could not sustain them. Each awakened new hope and its failure new disappointment.

I was attempting to pray the Liturgy of the Hours with little understanding of its history, theology, and spirituality and with no instruction in its chief component: the Psalms. I see now that the result was almost inevitable: I could choose to be faithful, could make the effort, and could experience some fruitfulness. But I could not dispel the sense of something missing, too routine, and unsatisfying in my prayer of the Hours.

NONETHELESS, THE FRUITFULNESS was real. Various "small" experiences come to mind. One Holy Saturday, I sat in the rectory chapel and prayed the Office of Readings. The afternoon before, I had celebrated the Good Friday service in the parish, and in a few hours, the Easter Vigil would begin. I read the ancient homily that depicts the encounter of the risen Christ with Adam: "Awake, O sleeper, and rise from the dead, and Christ will give you light."[6] In the homily, Christ tells Adam what he has done to set us free: "For your sake I, your God, became your son; I, the Lord, took the form of a slave; I, whose home is above the heavens, descended to the earth and beneath the earth. . . ." Then I read the concluding line: "The sword that pierced me has sheathed the sword that was turned against you." There I stopped: *The sword that was turned against you has been sheathed.* Christ himself has sheathed it. I sat in the chapel and felt my heart lift. My thoughts turned to Saint Paul's words to the Romans: "If God is for us, who can be against us?" (Rom 8:31).[7] I wrote in my journal: "Pray again with this homily and with Romans 8. I think this is very important, and I need to return to it."

In one diocese, my community staffed two rural parishes. I helped in the larger and was responsible for the smaller. One Friday, as was our custom, I prayed Morning Prayer with the people before Mass. I was still new to the parish and, in my first months there, had visited its families. Some lived in the town and others in farming hamlets scattered through the countryside. The impressions of those visits remained fresh in my heart. As we prayed, I thought of the financial difficulties, physical pain, troubled relationships, and struggling families I had encountered in those visits. I remembered, too, those far from faith and the Church.

We reached the canticle from Jeremiah 14. There the prophet voices his heartfelt sorrow at the plight of his people and cries out to the Lord for their healing: "Let my eyes stream with tears / day and night, without rest /. . . . If I walk out into the field, / look! those slain by the sword; / if I enter the city, look! those consumed by hunger /. . . . For your name's sake spurn us not, / disgrace not the throne of your glory" (Jer 14:17–18, 21).[8] As I read these words, I sensed Jeremiah's deep love for his people, his anguish at their suffering, and his plea for their healing. His sentiments became mine and gave me words to pray for my own people in their sufferings. Since then, whenever I pray this canticle in Morning Prayer, I remember what it meant to me that day.

On January 25, the Church celebrates the conversion of Saint Paul on the road to Damascus. One year, on that day, I read the homily of Saint John Chrysostom in the Office of Readings. The saint affirms that "Paul, more than anyone else, has shown us what man really is," and he then adds, "The most important thing of all to him . . . was that he knew himself to be loved by Christ."[9] I had read that line for many years. This year, the significance of these words struck me: Saint Paul perceived clearly the *most important thing* in his life, and this was that *he knew Christ loved him*. I thought of the many things I considered important in my life and toward which my thoughts often turned in hope or anxiety. And here was the most important of them all: *I am loved*. I am loved infinitely *by Christ*. From time to time, I recall Saint John Chrysostom's words. When I do, they remind me again of what matters most in my life.

Such moments were welcome. They did not change, however, my habitual pattern in praying the Hours: a sincere effort to be faithful, coupled, too often, with a sense of routine. More was necessary, and I did not know how to find it.

Chapter 3

Explorations

*How can I perceive His
presence within me? It is full
of life and efficacy, and no
sooner has He entered than my
sluggish soul is awakened.*
—St. Bernard of Clairvaux

FOR TWENTY YEARS of my priesthood, my spiritual director
was Jesuit father Ed O'Flaherty. Father Ed was a good man
with a warm heart, learned and prayerful, a sure spiritual
guide. I was one of many who felt his loss deeply when he
died of a brain tumor.

Periodically, I discussed with him my struggles with the
Liturgy of the Hours. Once I told him of a deacon I knew
who prayed the Liturgy of the Hours at length, stopping
where the words drew him. Father Ed said that, yes, the
Liturgy of the Hours may serve as a source of meditation.
He directed me, however, to the Liturgy of the Hours as
liturgical prayer and suggested that I learn more about its
nature and components. He encouraged me to deepen my
understanding of the Psalms. He explained that these may
be prayed in the person of Christ and cited as an example
Christ's prayer on the Cross, "My God, my God, why have
you forsaken me?" taken from Psalm 22.[1] He noted how
the Psalms may also be prayed in the name of the Church
and for the needs of its members. Father Ed advised, finally,

that I do some reading on the Liturgy of the Hours. Looking back, I am impressed by the theological and spiritual precision of his counsel.

A year later, we spoke once more of the Liturgy of the Hours and meditation. Again Father Ed recommended that I pray the Liturgy of the Hours according to its nature as the Church's liturgical prayer. A second time, he invited me to explore the Christian way of praying the Psalms, explaining that I could pray them from the perspective of Christ, of the Church, or of my personal situation.

In December of the following year, we returned to these matters a third time. We spoke during Advent, the time when the new liturgical year begins. Perhaps because of this, Father Ed shared a personal practice. Each Advent, he said, he tried to reread the *General Instruction of the Liturgy of the Hours* placed at the beginning of the breviary.[2] In this seventy-seven-page text, the Church explains the Liturgy of the Hours: its nature as a sharing in the eternal hymn of praise within the Trinity and as the prayer of Christ, Word made flesh, together with the Church he associates with himself; the role of the Holy Spirit in the Liturgy of the Hours; its character as a prayer for all in the Church; the place of the community in its celebration; the Liturgy of the Hours as a consecration of the entire day; the bond between the Liturgy of the Hours and the Eucharist; praise and petition in the Liturgy of the Hours; and so forth. The *Instruction* also describes each of the hours (Morning Prayer, Daytime Prayer, Evening Prayer, Night Prayer, and the Office of Readings) and explores their various elements: psalms and canticles, antiphons, hymns, readings from Scripture and the Church Fathers, intercessions, and the Our Father.

Father Ed told me that he reread this text each Advent to renew his prayer of the Liturgy of the Hours. It helped him, he said, to see if he was forgetting any dimensions of the Liturgy of the Hours and to understand again why he prayed it. When he read the *Instruction*, he added, he gained new insight into this prayer. As an example, he mentioned one year when he noted the difference between the invocations in Morning Prayer and the intercessions in Evening Prayer: the first ask for God's help during the day; the second seek God's assistance for various needs in the Church and world. Only later would I realize that Father Ed's precise counsel regarding the Hours arose from this yearly review of the *Instruction*.

I admired Father Ed's practice. His repeated reading emphasized the value of the *Instruction* for growth in praying the Liturgy of the Hours. Each Advent, I would see the *Instruction* in the breviary and would consider reading it. Yet in the twenty years that he guided me, I never did.

I esteemed his advice. I saw the wisdom of Father Ed's invitation to study the Psalms and learn how a Christian prays them. I understood, in some measure at least, the value of the *Instruction* for praying the Liturgy of the Hours fruitfully. My life was busy, however, with other concerns. Years passed . . . and I did none of the reading Father Ed suggested. My failure to follow his counsel was my greatest error regarding the Liturgy of the Hours in these forty years. And the heart of this error was my twenty-year delay in reading the *Instruction*. A prayerful reading or shared study of this document is, I now believe, the most effective means for growth in praying the Liturgy of the Hours.

AFTER ORDINATION, in accord with the charism of my community, I began to give Ignatian retreats. I soon realized that to guide these responsibly I needed to learn more about the discernment of spirits, a central theme in Saint Ignatius's *Spiritual Exercises*. I began to study his rules for the discernment of spirits and to speak about them in retreats.[3] Opportunities to teach these rules multiplied, and each time I taught them, I learned more about them.

Increasingly, I perceived their power to *set captives free* (Lk 4:18) from the burden of spiritual desolation and so to instill hope on the spiritual journey.[4]

Ignatius expects—and experience confirms—that all who love and seek the Lord will undergo times of spiritual desolation: times when they do not sense God's closeness and when they feel discouraged, without energy for prayer or service to others. Such desolation, he tells us, is a common tactic of our spiritual enemy. God in his love permits this, Ignatius says, because we grow through resisting such desolation. If we learn, therefore, to be aware of this discouraging tactic of the enemy, to understand it, and to reject it, we are *set free* to love and serve the Lord. The goal of Ignatius's rules is to foster such freedom.[5]

In his sixth rule, Ignatius counsels the person in desolation to "insist more upon prayer and meditation."[6] In the discouragement of desolation, we feel a disinclination to pray. Not only, Ignatius says, should we resist the temptation to abandon prayer, but we must "insist" upon prayer and meditation *even more* in times of desolation. Gradually, I discovered that the Liturgy of the Hours helped me do this.

One February morning, I rose, prepared for the day, and went to the rectory chapel to pray. The day before I had felt tired and alone, and my heart was still heavy as the new day began. I found meditation difficult and struggled even to want to pray. I was scheduled to say Mass an hour later and would have to give a homily. With this heaviness in my heart, I wondered how I would do it.

Overcoming some reluctance, I picked up the breviary and began Morning Prayer. As I prayed, I felt my spirits rise. I went on to the Office of Readings. That day the Church commemorated Saint Polycarp, bishop and martyr. I read of his courage in the face of martyrdom and of his final prayer: "Lord, almighty God . . . I bless you for judging me worthy of this day, this hour, so that in the company of the martyrs

I may share the cup of Christ, your anointed one, and so rise again to eternal life in soul and body, immortal through the power of the Holy Spirit. May I be received among the martyrs in your presence today as a rich and pleasing sacrifice."[7] As I read of his faith and resolve, I felt my spirits lift further. I left the chapel with new warmth in my heart, ready for the Mass and the day.

On another day, something similar occurred. The morning had been busy with teaching and spiritual direction. When late afternoon arrived, I was alone in my room, feeling isolated and too tired to work. I found myself eating food I did not need and attempting to escape the loneliness through a novel. As I did so, the heaviness in my heart increased. On my desk, however, was the breviary, still to be prayed. I took the volume in hand and began to say Daytime Prayer. Almost immediately I felt my heart lift. I found myself able to examine the desolation and make better choices in resisting it. Through that examination, I understood more clearly the nature of this desolation—how it had begun, how it had deepened through the afternoon, and how it had sought to discourage me. I perceived also the steps necessary to withstand it, both in the moment and any time this form of desolation might repeat.[8] That afternoon, too, praying the Liturgy of the Hours brought freedom from desolation.

In our community, we pray Evening Prayer together before supper. One day we did this as usual, but at the time, I was recovering from vocal surgery and speaking required effort. That evening I found saying the psalms and prayers more difficult than usual, and at supper one of the priests commented on this. His words touched the anxiety I already felt regarding my recovery and left me more anxious still. Supper ended, and I went to my evening tasks with this weight in my heart. Before retiring, I sat in the chapel for Night Prayer and the examen.[9] As I prayed Night Prayer, I felt the heaviness lighten: "In you O God, my body will rest in hope. . . . Preserve me, God, I take refuge in you. I say to the Lord: 'You are my God. My happiness lies in you. . . .' Into your hands, Lord, I commend my spirit. . . . Protect us Lord, as we stay awake; watch over us as we sleep. . . . Lord God, send peaceful sleep to refresh our tired bodies . . ."[10] The burden did not disappear entirely, but the desolation began to diminish, and I could see the issues more clearly.

As such experiences repeated, I came to see a pattern. In times of desolation, I would feel a reluctance to pray the Liturgy of the Hours. My nonreflective (undiscerning) tendency would be to delay or omit it. But as the hours of the day passed, there was the Liturgy of the Hours, its Daytime Prayer, Office of Readings, and Evening Prayer accumulating and waiting to be prayed. Finally, with some struggle, I would take the breviary and begin to pray the Hours. Usually the first minutes would be dry and difficult. Gradually, however, the prayer would become warmer. Frequently, praying the Liturgy of the Hours was the turning point between immersion in desolation and readiness to resist it. A prayer *of the hours*, rhythmically calling me to pray in times of desolation, proved a blessing, and I was grateful.

TEACHING IGNATIAN DISCERNMENT soon led to talks on Ignatian prayer as well. I spoke on Ignatian meditation (the reflective approach) and contemplation (the imaginative approach) of Scripture and on the examen prayer.[11]

In these presentations, I explored Ignatius's counsel regarding how to begin prayer. His text in the *Spiritual Exercises* reads, "A step or two before the place where I am about to contemplate or meditate, I will stand for the time it takes to say an Our Father, with my mind raised on high, considering how God our Lord looks upon me."[12] This, I noted, is a "threshold-of-prayer" exercise, and it is brief: "the time it takes to say an Our Father." I explained that during this space of an Our Father, persons about to pray focus on *what God is doing* as they enter prayer. What God is doing, Ignatius says, is *looking upon* them. And these persons are to consider, he specifies, *how* God looks upon them as they begin prayer.

In my teaching, I would ask, What do we see in the eyes of God as we enter prayer? How does God look upon us? We read in the Gospel of John that "no one has ever seen God" (Jn 1:18).[13] How then can we do what Ignatius asks? How can we know what we see in the eyes of God as we begin prayer?

I would answer this question in the light of the Incarnation—Jesus, God made flesh, God made visible (1Jn 1:1). John indeed tells us that "no one has ever seen God," but he immediately adds, "The only Son, God, who is at the Father's side, has revealed him" (Jn 1:18).[14] Consequently, I would say in my talks, this question may be rephrased as follows: "What did those who approached Jesus with humble and sincere hearts see in his eyes?"[15] What, for example, did the Samaritan woman see in Jesus' eyes when she met him at the well (Jn 4:1–26)? What did Levi see in Jesus' eyes when Jesus looked upon him at his tax-collector's bench (Mk 2:14)? What did the woman who washed Jesus' feet with her tears see in his eyes when he looked upon her (Lk 7:36–50)? What did Mary Magdalene see in Jesus' eyes when he pronounced her name on Easter morning (Jn 20:16)? What did Peter see in Jesus' eyes at the lakeside when Jesus asked three times if he loved him (Jn 21:15–19)? We would discuss these and similar encounters with Jesus. I would comment that throughout the Gospels, whenever people approached Jesus with goodwill, the love, warmth, and welcome they saw in his eyes won their hearts and transformed their lives. It is this look, I would conclude, that Ignatius invites us to see "for the time it takes to say an Our Father" as we enter prayer.

I taught this repeatedly to others. When I did, I suggested that this brief exercise might benefit not only our prayer

with Scripture but other times of prayer as well. After pro-
posing this for years to others, I finally realized that I could
do this before I prayed the Liturgy of the Hours.

I began to consider "how God our Lord looks upon me"
before each Hour as I prayed it. I chose scriptural verses to
help me, as, for example, "Jesus looking upon him loved
him" (Mk 10:21).[16] For the space of an Our Father, I would
see this loving look of Jesus directed personally toward me.
I found this made a great difference in praying the Liturgy
of the Hours. It changed the Hours from "something to be
done with fidelity" to a *relationship*: an encounter between
two persons. And once the Liturgy of the Hours became
relational, it became prayer.

Through this experience, I also learned that what happens *during* my prayer of the Hours depends significantly
on what happens *before* I begin this prayer.[17] I found that
this brief, unhurried pause to become aware of the Lord's
presence to me and love for me changed the way I prayed the
Liturgy of the Hours. Now as I prayed the hymns, psalms,
antiphons, readings, and invocations, I was listening to and
speaking to a Person.

Something else, unexpected but welcome, resulted from
this simple exercise. Beginning the Hours this way meant that
five times a day I consciously recalled the Lord's presence to
me and his love for me. As a result, I found it easier to do
this before other activities as well: before a time of exercise,
for example, or the preparation of a talk. I began to experience the Liturgy of the Hours as a true prayer *of the hours*:
a prayer that helped me find the Lord throughout the day, at
least in its principal moments. I began to understand the specific nature of the Liturgy of the Hours as a means of bring-
ing prayer into the entire day (Lk 18:1; 1Thess 5:17).

Here, too, as in the preceding chapter, I do not wish to
exaggerate. I still struggled with distractions and tiredness,
and even this brief pause before praying could be perfunctory

at times. It was impossible, however, to stop five times a day to remember that I was loved without something changing. The Liturgy of the Hours was beginning to feel like prayer.

WHEN I BEGAN WRITING, I was hosted by a college in Canada as a writer-in-residence. I was given an office in the college and a room with the religious community to which the college belonged. The community's house was large and well organized. Its members subscribed to many periodicals, and I enjoyed reading them. As I did, I learned about political, cultural, and religious situations in countries of which before then I had known little. The reading opened my eyes to the needs and struggles of nations in Eastern Europe, Latin America, Africa, Asia, and throughout the world.

The daily paper likewise informed me of events in the country where I was staying. Each morning, I had breakfast in the house before heading to the college. Most often I was alone for this meal and read the daily paper. Then, with renewed awareness of conditions in the world and locally, I would walk to the office, say Morning Prayer and the Office of Readings, and begin to write.

Over the months, the conjunction of these two things—a growing consciousness of the needs of the world and the Liturgy of the Hours—led to something new. I had long felt that I prayed too little for others. People would ask for prayers, and I would tell them sincerely that I would pray for them. I did pray for them, but a few days later, I would no longer remember their intentions. At times, others would tell me they prayed for me daily, and I would be grateful. But I seldom did the same and felt something missing.

Now I was praying Morning Prayer and the Office of Reading a few minutes after reading the news of the day and with an expanding awareness of nations around the world. Gradually, I realized that I could pray the Liturgy of the Hours for the specific needs of the world that day. I had always known that the Liturgy of the Hours was prayer for the Church and the world. That was a generic truth, however, and felt remote. This was specific. These needs had names, faces, and geographical locations. Prayer for them was necessary, and I welcomed the opportunity to offer that prayer.

I began by remembering these needs in Morning Prayer after the invocations. Before the Our Father that concludes them, I would stop, recall the situations of which I had read, and ask the Lord's help for them in the day just beginning. Later I chose one particular need and offered Morning Prayer as a whole for that intention. Still later, I extended this practice to all the Hours, praying each for specific persons or situations in the world. As I did so, the Liturgy of the Hours acquired new meaning. When I prayed it for a nation divided by war, the victims of a natural disaster, a person who was ill, a parishioner, a family member, or anyone who had asked my prayers, I wanted, in a new way, to pray it well. I wanted to contribute, through this prayer, to the outpouring of God's love and strength upon these persons. I began to find in the Liturgy of the Hours the answer to my sense that I prayed too little for others.

THE FOUNDER OF MY COMMUNITY, the Venerable Bruno Lanteri, asked his priests to give parish missions. These missions are retreats, usually of three to four days, held in a parish church for the people of that parish. Fifteen years after ordination, I met a Redemptorist priest who was a master of such missions. I was impressed by his skill, and to learn more about this ministry, I asked to join him in a parish mission.

It was unlike anything I had ever seen. Night after night, the church was filled to overflowing capacity. To accommodate the crowds, chairs were placed in the main aisle, and the choir loft was opened. The people loved this priest's manner of presentation and his message. One afternoon, during the mission, he explained to me how he prepared his talks. He showed me his files: clippings from newspapers and magazines, references from movies, works of literature, art, and so forth that made his message concrete for his hearers. When something struck him as useful for his talks, he copied it and placed it on file. I admired his practice and began to imitate it. With time, I extended this to the Liturgy of the Hours as well. I focused above all on the second reading of the Office of Readings: the writings, for example, of Saint Augustine, Saint Ignatius of Antioch, Saint Gregory the Great, Saint Basil, Saint Teresa of Avila, Saint John of the Cross, and many others. When a passage especially appealed to me, I copied and filed it.

Some years later, I offered a retreat on prayer for laity. In the conferences, I explored texts on prayer from Saint Augustine, Saint John Chrysostom, Saint Colomban, Saint Anselm, Jean-Pierre de Caussade, Saint Jean Vianney, and Romano Guardini. The group maintained silence throughout the weekend and then, on Sunday morning, gathered for a sharing of graces. When they did, several retreatants mentioned how they welcomed the readings from these spiritual figures. In their writings, they found nourishment and discovered a tradition of Christian sanctity they wished to pursue further.

After that weekend, I thought about their comments. One text we had read was a passage from Saint Anselm that I found apt for retreats: "O little man, escape from your everyday business for a short while, hide for a moment from your restless thoughts. Break off from your cares and troubles and be less concerned about your tasks and labors. Make a little time for God and rest awhile in him."[18] In another, Saint Augustine taught, "The entire life of a good Christian is in fact an exercise of holy desire. You do not yet see what you long for, but the very act of desiring prepares you, so that when he comes you may see and be utterly satisfied."[19] In yet another, Saint Jean Vianney spoke to his parishioners of prayer: "My little children, your hearts are small, but prayer stretches them and makes them capable of God. Through prayer we receive a foretaste of heaven and something of paradise comes down upon us."[20] In still another, Saint Bernard reflected on the saints and shared a personal longing: "I tell you that when I think of them, I feel myself inflamed by a tremendous yearning."[21]

I was happy to introduce the retreatants to these spiritual masters, many of whom were new to them. Through their eyes, I grasped anew the richness of these spiritual writings, and my gratitude for this resource in my ministry deepened. Then as I reflected, I realized that I owed most of this to the Liturgy of the Hours. The greater part of the texts I had shared I had first read in the Office of Readings.

On my own, I read the Church Fathers only occasionally. Day after day, however, in the Liturgy of the Hours, I encountered them and learned from their wisdom. The comments of the retreatants revealed to me a gift received from the Liturgy of the Hours: it mediated to me the treasures of the Church's centuries-old spiritual tradition. These treasures blessed both me and my ministry.

As the years passed, in varying and complementary ways I began to find meaning in the Liturgy of the Hours. These insights, however, had not yet touched its core—its specific nature as the Church's *liturgical* prayer of the hours. This was a truth yet to be explored.

Chapter 4

Foundations

Prayer demands intelligence.
The Psalms bring our hearts
and minds into the presence of
the living God. They fill our
minds with His Truth in order
to unite us with His Love.
—Thomas Merton[1]

IN SEPTEMBER OF my thirty-first year of priesthood, I made my annual retreat. This pause in my activity was welcome, even urgent. My ministry of public speaking had grown, requiring constant travel throughout the year. At the same time, I was working intensely on a demanding writing project. My mother's health also had deteriorated. To help her as I could, I spent some months each year in a parish near her, continuing my work and spending time with her. Those were precious months for which I will always be grateful. The combination of these activities, however, led to deep tiredness.

My director wisely counseled that I slow the pace during the retreat. As the quiet days unfolded, I saw my need for change. The productive but exhausting way I was living was unsustainable. I had to place communion with the Lord at the center of my life and let the activity flow from there. I needed to trust that less activity, springing from physical and spiritual health, would be more fruitful than the

strenuous life I was living. I came to see this as *deliber-
ate slowness*: the choice to attend prudently to physical and
spiritual needs so as to better serve the Lord.

During the retreat, this realization deepened. As it did, it
impacted my prayer of the Liturgy of the Hours. Each day
during the retreat, I prayed the five Hours. When I prayed
them, I deliberately slowed the recitation. Before praying a
psalm, I took time to read the psalm title and introductory
sentence. After the psalm, I prayed the optional psalm prayer.
I said parts of the Hours out loud. I read the long scriptural
reading from my Bible, sometimes adding the omitted verses.

When I prayed it this way, I found that I liked the Liturgy
of the Hours. It felt increasingly like *prayer*. The slower
recitation added only a few minutes to the Hours, but those
minutes made a great difference. They changed the Liturgy
of the Hours from something to recite and finish to a prayer
in which I was taking initiative.

After the retreat, I reflected on this experience. I saw that
the decision to pray the Liturgy of the Hours with deliber-
ate slowness required a *surrender* to it. Years earlier, I had
seen that the fundamental choice regarding the Liturgy of
the Hours was whether or not I would pray it. Now I realized that, though I was praying the Liturgy of the Hours,
I still needed to surrender to it—to be willing to pray it
without hurry, according to its nature, and with attention
to its various parts. When I did, I found that I liked it and
experienced it as nourishing.

Once more, I do not wish to exaggerate. My prayer of
the Liturgy of the Hours did not change overnight. Times
of tiredness and distraction continued, days when the Hours
again felt like "something to do and to finish." But the surrender was new and opened a way to enter the Liturgy of
the Hours more deeply.

*   *   *

TWO YEARS LATER, I decided to refresh my grasp of the Liturgy of the Hours. I determined finally to do what Father Ed had counseled so many years earlier: to read the *General Instruction of the Liturgy of the Hours*. I chose also to reread Father Raffa's book on the theology of the Liturgy of the Hours.[2] These two sources, I thought, would be sufficient. I expected to complete the reading quickly, since I thought I had assimilated this material years earlier.

I began reading the *General Instruction*. In the breviary from which I read it, the text by which Pope Paul VI approved the renewed Liturgy of the Hours precedes the *Instruction*.[3] The pope's first sentence caught my attention: "The hymn of praise that is sung through all the ages in the heavenly places and was brought by the high priest, Christ Jesus, into this land of exile has been continued by the Church with constant fidelity over many centuries, in a rich variety of forms."[4] The *Instruction* explained that "when the Church offers praise to God in the Liturgy of the Hours it unites itself with that hymn of praise."[5]

Questions immediately arose in my mind. Of what hymn of praise did the pope speak? Is there a hymn of praise sung through all ages in the heavenly places? Who sings it? In what does it consist? If this hymn is sung through all ages— that is, eternally—then it must be sung within the Trinity. Is there, then, an eternal hymn of praise within the Trinity? Do the Persons of the Trinity praise each other through all ages? How should I understand the pope's words?

This was clearly holy ground, deep in the mystery of the Trinity, and had to be approached with reverence. But I knew that Paul VI had said something fundamental about the Liturgy of the Hours, something I needed to explore if I wanted to grow in understanding it. His first sentence alone opened perspectives on the Liturgy of the Hours that I had never considered.

As I continued to read, I learned that the Liturgy of the Hours is essentially a prayer of praise. I had prayed the Hours for almost forty years, and yet this was new to me. Prayers of thanksgiving, contrition, and petition were familiar to me. I knew what it meant to thank God for blessings received, to express sorrow for sin and failings, and to ask God's help for many needs, my own and those of others. But what did it mean to *praise* God? I had no clear answer. Why did God want my praise? Again I did not know. And why was this the essential focus of the Liturgy of the Hours? Once more, I had no reply. In retrospect, it amazes me that I prayed the Liturgy of the Hours for so many years without considering these questions and without realizing their importance. For decades I had said prayers of praise with goodwill but with no understanding of praise itself. And this was the key element of the Liturgy of the Hours. . . .

In my reading, I noted that the psalms are Jewish prayers. Further questions arose: Why was I, a Christian, praying Jewish prayers? Why was I reciting prayers filled with references to Israel, Jerusalem, the Mosaic Law, and sacrifices of animals?

The *Instruction* showed me that the New Testament writers and Church Fathers saw Christ in the Psalms and that the Liturgy of the Hours does as well. When Father Ed had said this to me years earlier, I had heard his words without grasping their significance. Now I wondered: How was I to see Christ in Psalms written centuries before his birth? What did this mean for how I prayed the Psalms?

My reading told me that psalms may be prayed in different ways. A psalm, for example, that pleads for deliverance from foes may be understood to express Christ's prayer in his Passion. Prayed this way, it offers insight into his heart and experience. The same psalm may be prayed on behalf of the Church, invoking God's aid for her suffering members in the world. It may also be prayed for God's help in personal struggles.

When, for example, I prayed Psalm 57, a cry to God in a time of anguish—"Have mercy on me, God. . . . My soul

lies down among lions, who would devour the sons of men.
Their teeth are spears and arrows, their tongue a sharpened
sword. . . . They laid a snare for my steps, my soul was
bowed down"—I could hear these words as Christ's prayer
to his Father during his Passion.[6] I could also pray them
for any in the Church and the world suffering anguish that
day. Finally, this psalm provided a way to beg God's help
in personal struggles. If my reading raised questions I could
not answer, it also opened entirely new ways of praying the
Liturgy of the Hours.

I had long assumed that I understood the theology of the
Liturgy of the Hours and so knew how to pray it. Now I
was startled to see how little I really knew and how much I
had to learn. I was humbled to find myself unable to answer
even basic questions about the Liturgy of the Hours. When I
finished the *Instruction* and Father Raffa's book, I asked to
speak with a professor of liturgy and discussed these questions with him. That conversation clarified much; it also
indicated further sources to explore, and I began to read
them as well. At this point, I realized that my reading had
become a significant new step on the journey. For the first
time in forty years, I was consciously seeking formation in
the Liturgy of the Hours.

I began to understand Father Ed's counsel given so long
ago. I saw why he had urged me to read the *General Instruction*: it is the fundamental text for understanding the Liturgy
of the Hours, to which all other writing refers. The first
part of the *Instruction*, more theological in nature, deepened
my understanding of the Liturgy of the Hours. The second,
more practical part, to my surprise—and, to be honest, my
chagrin—answered many of my earlier objections to the
Liturgy of the Hours. I found that most of them had been
foreseen and resolved in the *Instruction*. The problem was
that I had never read it! At times, for example, I had resisted
the omitting of verses from the scriptural reading, preferring

the full text as found in the Bible. Thinking it rebellion, I had used my Bible with the unabridged text rather than that given in the breviary. Now I read the discussion of these scriptural readings in the *Instruction* and found this: "One may laudably read them in full from an approved text [Bible]."[7] When I read that sentence, I had to smile, somewhat ruefully. What impressed me here as throughout the *Instruction* was its flexibility and the many options it provided to render the Liturgy of the Hours truly prayer.[8]

THE INSTRUCTION TOLD ME that the Liturgy of the Hours is primarily a prayer of *praise*. As mentioned, this was new for me. I had seldom thought of praising God and did not understand why this was so important, even the central focus of the Hours. Praise, I thought, was a form of prayer privileged by some and associated with expressive gestures and gospel music. Charismatics praised God. Praise and worship music praised God. In Hispanic ministry, I had encountered warm and compelling prayers of praise. I respected and liked such prayer; but it was not my habitual form of prayer. As I reflected, I realized that I had always centered my prayer of the Hours on two things: *meditation* on the content of the psalms and readings and *petition* for various needs. I had never thought of the Liturgy of the Hours as a prayer of praise.

Now I saw that praise situates us in our truth as creatures before our Creator and as those redeemed before our Redeemer. I never doubted that I was God's creature and that Christ had redeemed me. My awareness of this, however, would often fade in the busyness of the day. I could easily lose sight of God and of who I am before him.

As I read, I found that praise is the way to *live* in the truth that I am God's creature, loved before all ages, given life in time, and called to eternal joy and that praise is the way to *live* in the truth that I am loved infinitely by the Redeemer, who gave his life for me. One quotation expressed this best for me. Praise is, the author said, "essentially an unlimited appreciation of the grandeur of God, a loving appreciation which expresses itself in words, and better still in song. It is not a cold and objective statement, but warm and human acknowledgement of God."[9] When I understood praise as loving appreciation and warm and human acknowledgment of God, I found it inviting. I found that I wanted to praise God.

When I saw this, the Liturgy of the Hours changed for me from black and white to color. It came alive. For the first time, I noticed that the very beginning of each Hour centers on praise: "Glory be to the Father, the Son, and the Holy Spirit," and "Alleluia." The hymns praise God: "I sing the mighty power of God," "Praise the Lord ye heavens adore him," and many like hymns.[10] The psalms and canticles praise God: "I will praise you, Lord, you have rescued me," "Praise the Lord from the heavens," "Alleluia. Salvation, glory, and power to our God," and many others.[11] The Gospel canticles of Zechariah and Mary praise God: "Blessed be the Lord, the God of Israel," and "My soul proclaims the greatness of the Lord."[12] I saw that praise was indeed primary in the Liturgy of the Hours.[13]

One evening during the writing of this book, I sat in my room and began to pray Night Prayer. I read the words of the hymn: "We praise you, Father, for your gifts, of dusk and nightfall over earth."[14] I thought of how this praise, offered in so ordinary a setting and with its limitations of tiredness and distraction, is raised by the Holy Spirit to Jesus, who joins it to his prayer and that of the entire Church, his Mystical Body, and so presents it to his Father, uniting it with "the hymn of praise that is sung through all the ages" in the loving communion of the Trinity. As I reflected, I began to understand the power of the Liturgy of the Hours and how "our meager prayer," as one friend calls it, gains richness and beauty through the gift of the Triune God and so blesses the world.

On another day, I prayed Psalm 66 in the Office of Readings. I read the first verse: "Cry out with joy to God all the earth, O sing to the glory of his name. O render him glorious praise. Say to God, 'How tremendous your deeds!'"[15] I directed these words to Jesus, finding that this made the prayer more concrete and relational. As I did, I felt my heart grow warm with an awareness of God's deeply personal love. Such experiences help me understand why God desires my praise: something blessed enters my life when I praise him.

IN FOUR DECADES of praying the Liturgy of the Hours, I had never studied the Psalms. I had never felt the need. Now that changed. As I learned more about this prayer, I saw more clearly my weak background in the Psalms. I had no instruction in them, and they were the chief component of the Liturgy of the Hours!

In all these years, I had never explored the Christian meaning of the Psalms. As a result, I could pray them only according to their literal, Old Testament meaning. Some psalms were accessible to me on this level. Those that expressed personal experience—sorrow, need, hope, and joy—spoke directly to me, and I could pray them. Others, however, contained explicitly Old Testament themes and seemed to apply less to my life: "The Lord shatters the cedars of Lebanon; he makes Lebanon leap like a calf and Sirion like a young wild-ox" (Ps 29); "In your goodness, show favor to Zion: rebuild the walls of Jerusalem. Then you will be pleased with lawful sacrifice, holocausts offered on your altar" (Ps 51).[16] I prayed these psalms with goodwill, but they were distant in time and culture. Some expressions—"My vows to the Lord I will fulfill before all his people. O precious in the eyes of the Lord is the death of his faithful" (Ps 116:14–15)—I prayed for years without understanding them.[17]

Now I learned that the Psalms, like the Old Testament as a whole, find their fulfillment in Christ (Lk 24:44). The New Testament writers, the Fathers, and the Church through the ages, therefore, understood the Psalms to speak about Christ.[18] I was free, then, to see Christ in them and to pray them to Christ.

For years I had wished to pray the Psalms to Jesus and at times did so. I was never entirely sure, however, about the theological correctness of this practice. When a psalm said, for example, "O God, you are my God, for you I long" (Ps 63:1), it was addressed to the one God of Israel.[19] Could I, as a Christian, speak these words to Christ? Was this theologically proper? Now I understood that I could indeed say these words to Christ and that, in fact, the Psalms find their fullness in Christ. When I saw this, the Psalms themselves acquired a new relational quality: their words offered a way to converse with Christ and to share with him my hopes and fears, burdens and desires.

Something similar occurred with the Church. I had often read, for example, the words of Psalm 137: "By the rivers of Babylon, there we sat and wept, remembering Zion."[20] This psalm helped me reverence the sorrow of Israel in its exile and its yearning for Jerusalem. But this was remote: I was a contemporary Christian, not an Israelite in exile centuries before Christ.

My reading now taught me that the New Jerusalem, the New Israel, was the Church, the People of God inaugurated by Christ. Once I saw this, the psalms that spoke of Israel's needs, sufferings, and hopes gained new meaning. I could pray these psalms for the needs and struggles of the New Israel, the Church in our world today. As one commentary said of Psalm 137, "The Christian prays the psalm as an expression of longing for the new Jerusalem, the Church, and for its renewal in time of disaster."[21] An inviting approach to praying these psalms, too, began to unfold.

Learning about the psalms also changed my perspective on singing the Liturgy of the Hours. I had never fully grasped that the Psalms are *songs*. When I did, my interest in singing the Psalms grew: I wanted to experience the Psalms in their full and original setting. I began to attend, for example, to the singing of the responsorial psalm at Sunday Mass. This seemed the fullest setting for a psalm: the liturgy, a church, an assembly gathered for worship, musical instruments, and a cantor leading the singing of the congregation. I also saw with new eyes the singing of psalms in our community prayer. On Sundays or special feasts, we sang the hymn, the psalms, and the Gospel canticle. The melodies for the psalms were simple, repetitive, and easily learned. I noted how the singing slowed the recitation and so facilitated greater assimilation. It helped unite us as a community in prayer. Here, too, I experienced the Psalms in their full setting: songs of praise sung by an assembly in liturgical prayer.

I found that singing the Psalms also required the surrender to the Liturgy of the Hours mentioned previously: I had to accept the slower pace and added minutes in prayer. Sometimes—when in a hurry or when feeling desolate—this required some effort. Yet if I did make this surrender, the singing enriched the prayer.

THIS PROCESS OF LEARNING about the Liturgy of the Hours is still incomplete. I am only beginning to explore the individual psalms. I have much to learn about the role of the Holy Spirit in the Liturgy of the Hours. Saint Paul's teaching that "the Spirit helps us in our weakness; for we do not know how to pray as we ought" and that "the Spirit himself intercedes for us with sighs too deep for words" (Rom 8:26) reveals to me depths in the Liturgy of the Hours of which I know little.[22] Likewise, when Saint Augustine writes of Christ that "he prays for us as our priest, he prays in us as our head, [and] he is the object of our prayer as our God," so that we "hear our voices in his voice, and his voice in ours," I struggle to grasp these truths and to apply them to my prayer of the Hours.[23]

I understand only inadequately the relationship between the Mass and the Liturgy of the Hours. The Second Vatican Council teaches that the Mass is the "source and summit" of Christian life.[24] The Liturgy of the Hours, the *Instruction* says, "extends to the different hours of the day the praise and thanksgiving, the commemoration of the mysteries of salvation, the petitions and the foretaste of heavenly glory that are present in the Eucharistic mystery."[25] Two images help me approach this truth: a jewel set in a case that enhances its beauty and the sun that sheds its rays throughout the day.[26] The Mass is the "jewel" that Christ has given to his Spouse, the Church; the Liturgy of the Hours reflects and extends its beauty through the hours of the day. The Mass is the "sun" that radiates its grace upon the Liturgy of the Hours as the day unfolds. These images assist me, but I have not assimilated this relationship enough in practice. I hope to pursue this truth more deeply in the future.

"Prayer demands intelligence." I understand now how these words apply to the Liturgy of the Hours. Years ago, Father Ed sought to guide me to that "intelligence," that accurate understanding that enriches the prayer of the Hours. Though I waited too long, I am glad to have begun, at least, this journey.

Chapter 5

Journey

On this road we must always
keep walking if we are to arrive.
—Saint John of the Cross

THIS ACCOUNT ENDS in midstream, forty years after it began. The journey is still incomplete. These years have brought growth but have not eliminated all struggle. At times, I allow myself to become too tired, and the quality of my prayer diminishes. When discouraged, I may delay the Hours until late afternoon or evening. Even in the best of times, prayer requires attention, and I may accept that effort reluctantly. As I learn more about the Liturgy of the Hours, I see more clearly the gap between what I understand and how I actually pray.

But I know these efforts to grow matter. A deeper grasp of the Liturgy of the Hours increases my esteem for it. I find that I desire it more. In Ignatian terms, these efforts *dispose* me to receive the *gift* of prayer in the Liturgy of the Hours.

A friend who has prayed the Liturgy of the Hours for many years says, "I think that the majority of people who pray the Liturgy of the Hours do so after much labor. I don't think its appreciation is immediate, nor am I wondering if it's supposed to be. Because I think that as you mature, not only physically but also spiritually, the Liturgy of the Hours is more and more appealing. It's almost a way of expressing that maturing relationship with Christ. That doesn't take place quickly, nor does praying the Liturgy of the Hours take place quickly."[1] I think my friend is right, both about the need for time and labor and about the increasing appeal of the Liturgy of the Hours when that persevering effort is accepted.

A woman in her early seventies has prayed the Liturgy of the Hours all her adult life. She says, "I have prayed the Psalms for years, but now it's different. When I began, I was praying the words of others. That was good. But now it is my own experience that I am expressing in praying the Psalms."[2] A priest, a deeply spiritual man, also prayed the Liturgy of the Hours faithfully throughout his life. In a letter written shortly before his death, he told a friend, "Imagine, I am just now discovering the beauty of the psalms: they speak to us only of the mercy of God."[3] *They speak only of the mercy of God*: I read these words decades ago and never forgot them. But now I begin, at least, to glimpse their meaning. I think this priest is right: most deeply, the psalms are the cry of human helplessness to God and the expression of human joy in the sure hope of that divine help—*they speak only of the mercy of God*. Persons like this woman and this priest are witnesses for me. They show me that more lies ahead on this road if I will keep walking.

WHILE I WAS WRITING this book, I traveled to a retreat center to guide a retreat. Near the center was a Benedictine monastery where the monks prayed the Liturgy of the Hours daily. A retreatant encouraged me to attend their prayer, telling me how much he had enjoyed it over the years. My interest awakened, and I willingly agreed.

The next morning, I left the center at 5:45 A.M. and walked to the monastery church. It was March, dark and cold. The moon was visible, and the stars could still be seen. Dawn was near. All was quiet, and the only sound was the singing of a few birds.

I entered the church. It was large and Romanesque in style. The long nave was still dark, and only the choir stalls were lit as, one by one, the monks arrived. At 6:00 A.M., they began to pray Vigils, the first of the Hours in the monastic day. The monks sang Psalm 95, the call to praise, repeating the antiphon, "O that today you would listen to his voice!"[4] After the psalm, they sat as one monk approached the ambo and, in a deep, unhurried voice, proclaimed the reading from Scripture. The text was Genesis 24, the encounter of Abraham's servant with Rebecca, the future wife of Jacob.

The reader finished and returned to his place. For several minutes, the monks sat quietly, reflecting on the Scripture they had heard. The soft sound of running water in the baptismal font and the low hum of the heating system formed a backdrop to the silence. Gradually, as the sun rose, the church was filling with light.

Then the monks stood. Again they prayed a psalm, this time Psalm 55, the prayer of one betrayed by a false friend. A second time, a monk proclaimed a text of Scripture: Jeremiah 24, the parable of the baskets of figs that symbolize responses of fidelity or infidelity to God's plan for his people. After this second reading, Vigils concluded. The monks left the church and returned to the monastery. In their measured walk and quiet calm, I sensed the familiarity of this routine in their lives. A half hour later, they would return to the church for Morning Prayer.

I walked back to the center. The sun had risen, and many birds were singing. I could hear the sounds of traffic in the distance. Twenty minutes later, after a quick breakfast, I returned to the church. Now it was filled with sunlight and revealed in its beauty. This was the hour for Morning Prayer—Lauds, as the monks termed it. We had prayed before dawn and were about to pray a second time in the early morning. I realized that for these men, this was truly a liturgy *of the hours*: periodic returns to prayer as cosmic time unfolded through the day.

I took the volume for prayer in hand. A monk noticed my efforts to find the pages and approached me. He explained that I would not find the hymn in that book because they would use a different one that day. This brief interaction made me feel less an observer and more a participant in the prayer. His thoughtfulness warmed me as we prepared to pray.

At 7:00 A.M., the church bells rang, and to the accompaniment of the organ, the monks sang the opening hymn. They chanted five psalms and canticles. All knew the melodies well and sang easily, without strain. No single voice emerged; all were joined in a united chant. The simplicity of the melodies allowed me to sing without difficulty.

Then all sat, as one monk read from Luke 12: "'Teacher, tell my brother to share the inheritance with me. . . .' Then he told them a parable. 'There was a rich man whose land produced a bountiful harvest. . . .' And he said, 'This is what I shall do: I shall tear down my barns and build larger ones. . . . And I shall say to myself . . . "eat, drink, and be merry!"' But God said to him, 'You fool, this night your life will be demanded of you.' . . . Thus will it be for the one who stores up treasure for himself but is not rich in what matters to God'" (Lk 12:13–21).[5]

As at Vigils, a time of quiet and reflection followed the reading. Again the church was silent except for the soft sounds of running water, the heating system, and an occasional cough. I felt the power of that moment. We had heard Jesus say that the key issue in life is *to be rich in what matters to God*. Everything in that setting—the austerity and beauty of the church, the witness of men dedicated to the monastic life, the time to reflect on Jesus' words after hearing them proclaimed, and the silence that allowed them to penetrate—moved me to say, Yes, that's right. That's obvious. The most important thing in our lives *is* to be rich in what matters to God.

The monks stood and, accompanied by the organ, sang the response to the reading: "O God, you are my God, at dawn I seek you." Led by the organ, they sang the antiphon to the Canticle of Zechariah: "Let us serve the Lord in holiness all the days of our life." As I listened, peace entered my heart. The prayer, simplicity, and beauty of that moment stirred me, slowed me, and lifted my heart. I felt that I was sharing in something holy. To know that, wherever I might be, these Hours would be prayed daily in this church, gave me a sense of surety, of calm assurance in my faith. It lightened my concerns and readied me for the day.

The remainder of the morning and afternoon was busy, filled with conferences and meetings with retreatants. Then at 5:30 P.M., I returned for Evening Prayer. Now the sun was setting, and during the prayer, the church gradually darkened. As the monks sang, read, and prayed in silence, again I felt peace fill my heart. For them, this prayer was a "given," almost a routine of every day. It was the staple of their spiritual life. I felt the privilege of sharing, if only for a day, in a centuries-old tradition: the rhythmic praying of the psalms in community to sanctify the hours of the day.

Later, I thought about this experience. As I did, I noted the similarity of this day with that spent earlier among the university students. These vocations—laymen and laywomen and Benedictine religious—were different, but in both settings, the beauty and richness of the Liturgy of the Hours were present. Both the day with the monks and the day with students had revealed to me new depths in the Liturgy of the Hours. I understood afresh why the Church insists that the Liturgy of the Hours is *for all*: Benedictines in their monastic churches, priests in their parishes, deacons in their active service, consecrated men and women in their many ministries, and laity—young and old, men and women, single or married—as they fulfill their God-given calling in the world today.[6]

Contemplative monks and nuns will pray it in the ordered life that permits regular gatherings for communal recitation of the Hours. Parish priests will pray it in the quiet morning hours as the day begins, in a moment snatched from busyness at midday, in a half hour before supper and evening meetings, and for a few tired minutes as the day ends. Deacons will pray it in the morning and evening and at other times should their bishops so direct or their devotion move them. Active religious will pray the Hours together or individually, in part or in whole, as their rules prescribe. Laypersons may pray Morning Prayer upon rising or listen to it commuting to work or heading to the supermarket. Families may pray a shortened form of Evening Prayer around the supper table, and husband and wife may pray Night Prayer together as the day closes.

All who pray it will experience the struggles and the fruit of this prayer. Persevering through the struggles, they will find the fruit increase until the Liturgy of the Hours becomes a cherished friend. To each the richness of the Liturgy of the Hours belongs. For all it may become a treasured source of spiritual strength.

ONE SIMPLE EXPERIENCE symbolizes for me how the Liturgy of the Hours blesses my life. In my community, we begin the day with Morning Prayer at 6:30 A.M. In the winter months, the mornings are dark and cold. The church may be cold as well. At times, I am alert during that prayer; at other times, I carry the fatigue of previous days' labor.

We sing the opening hymn and then sit to recite the psalms, one side of the church alternating with the other. When these conclude, we stand and sing the Canticle of Zechariah, offer the intentions of prayer, say the Our Father, and end with the final prayer. Some remain in church for the 7:00 A.M. Mass. Those who will celebrate later Masses leave the church together. Usually, three or four of us meet as one of us unlocks the door to the residence.

This is when we exchange our first greetings of the day. We may also hold brief conversations about matters of the day. Often something humorous is said, and we go to our tasks with a smile.

That is how the day begins. We pray the Liturgy of the Hours together. Then, blessed by this spiritual sharing, we share humanly as well. As we head to our various activities, the morning is no longer cold and dark, and we are ready for the day.

I am grateful that the Liturgy of the Hours has been part of my life for forty years. And I am grateful that it will accompany me on the road that lies ahead.

For Further Reading

Brook, John. *The School of Prayer: An Introduction to the Divine Office for All Christians*. Collegeville, MN: Liturgical, 1992. (A valuable tool for praying the Liturgy of the Hours.)

John Paul II. *Psalms and Canticles: Meditations and Catechesis on the Psalms and Canticles of Morning Prayer*. Chicago: Liturgical Training, 2004.

John Paul II and Benedict XVI. *Psalms and Canticles: Meditations and Catechesis on the Psalms and Canticles of Evening Prayer*. London: Catholic Truth Society, 2006.

Martimort, Aimé Georges. "The Liturgy of the Hours," in A. G. Martimort, ed., *The Church at Prayer*, vol. 4: *The Liturgy and Time*, 151–275. Collegeville, MN: Liturgical, 1986.

Merton, Thomas. *Praying the Psalms*. Collegeville, MN: Liturgical, 1956.

Scotto, Dominic, T.O.R. *Lord, Teach Us How to Pray: A Companion to the Liturgy of the Hours*. Staten Island, NY: Alba House, 2007.

Sockey, Daria. *The Everyday Catholic's Guide to the Liturgy of the Hours*. Cincinnati, OH: Servant, 2013.

United States Conference of Catholic Bishops. *General Instruction of the Liturgy of the Hours*. Washington, DC: author, 2009. (Also available online at various websites. This is the primary source for understanding the Liturgy of the Hours.)

Notes

Introduction

1. Timothy Gallagher, O.M.V., *The Discernment of Spirits: An Ignatian Guide to Everyday Living* (New York: Crossroad, 2005), and *Spiritual Consolation: An Ignatian Guide to the Greater Discernment of Spirits* (New York: Crossroad, 2007).

2. I refer here to Saint Ignatius's first set of rules for the discernment of spirits: *Spiritual Exercises*, 313–27. For the author's translation of this text, see Gallagher, *The Discernment of Spirits*, 7–10.

3. The renewal of the Liturgy of the Hours in the early 1970s generated a series of books and articles. Since then, less has been produced. More writing on the theology and spirituality of the Liturgy of the Hours is necessary in general and, in particular, in English.

Prologue: What Is the Liturgy of the Hours?

1. Mt 21:16; Mt 22:44; Mk 14:26; Mk 15:34; Lk 23:46; etc. Saint Ambrose writes, "In the psalms, then, not only is Jesus born for us, he also undergoes his saving passion in his body, he lies in death, he rises again, he ascends into heaven, he sits at the right hand of the Father." Office of Readings, Friday, Tenth Week in Ordinary Time, Second Reading, *The Liturgy of the Hours*, vol. 3 (New York: Catholic Book, 1975), 344.

2. *The Liturgy of the Hours*, vol. 1, 1056–59. All psalms cited in this paragraph are taken from this volume.

3. Office of Readings, Saturday, Tenth Week in Ordinary Time, Second Reading, *The Liturgy of the Hours*, vol. 3, 347–48.

4. Office of Readings, August 21, Second Reading, *The Liturgy of the Hours*, vol. 4, 1337.

5. Ibid.

6. "From at least the middle of the fourth century on, testimonies abound which mention or describe these daily assemblies, not only in Palestine, but at Antioch and Constantinople and in Africa. When St. John Chrysostom instructed the newly baptized of

Antioch he told them that these gatherings were a necessary part of a Christian day. The Spanish and Gallican councils of the fifth and sixth centuries frequently regulated the details of the assemblies or recommended that the faithful attend them." Aimé Georges Martimort, ed., *The Church at Prayer: An Introduction to the Liturgy* (Collegeville, MN: Liturgical, 1986), 171. "In the Fourth Century, everywhere in the various churches a service of morning and evening prayer was established in which the Christian people and the clergy took part. This institution is documented both in the Eastern and Western Church." Vincenzo Raffa, P.O.D.P., *La liturgia delle ore: Presentazione storica, teologica, e pastorale,* 3rd ed. (Milano: Edizioni O.R., 1990), 65. Author's translation.

7. For these details, see George Cuiver, C.R., *Company of Voices: Daily Prayer and the People of God* (Norwich, England: Canterbury, 2001), 52–53; Martimort, *The Church at Prayer,* 170–72.

8. A visitor to the parish of Saint Jean Vianney, the Curé d'Ars (1786–1859), described a typical Sunday afternoon and evening in the parish church: "M. le Curé gave catechism at one o'clock in the afternoon; the attendance at it was hardly less than at Mass. Vespers were followed by Compline. Then came the recitation of the rosary, in which everybody joined. At nightfall the bell rang out a third summons to church, and a third time the parish answered its call. At that hour M. Vianney left his confessional, recited night prayers and concluded the exercises of the day with one of those touching homilies to which I used to listen with so much pleasure." Francis Trochu, *The Curé d'Ars: St. Jean-Marie-Baptiste Vianney (1786–1859) According to the Acts of the Process of Canonization and Numerous Hitherto Unpublished Documents* (London: Burns Oates and Washbourne, 1951), 222. What I—following Cuiver (see the preceding note)—call the "people's office" is often designated the "cathedral office."

9. Prior to the Second Vatican Council, the Hours of the Divine Office were Matins, Lauds, Prime (6:00 A.M.), Terce (9:00 A.M.), Sext (12:00 P.M.), None (3:00 P.M.), Vespers, and Compline. A guest at a French Benedictine monastery in 1953 describes these Hours: "The monks' day, I learned, began at 4 a.m., with the offices of Matins and Lauds, followed by periods for private masses and reading and meditation. A guest's day began at 8:15 with the office of Prime and breakfast in silence. At 10 the Conventual High Mass was sandwiched between Tierce and Sext. Luncheon at 1. Nones and Vespers at 5 p.m. Supper at 7:30, then at 8:30, Compline and to bed in silence at 9." Patrick Leigh Fermor, *A Time to Keep Silence* (New York: New York Review, 2007), 12.

10. Martimort, *The Church at Prayer*, 157ff.

11. The further title "breviary" refers to the book itself of the Liturgy of the Hours in the shortened (Latin *brevis*) form given it after the Council of Trent. "Breviary" at times is used as a synonym of "Liturgy of the Hours" and "Divine Office" but is theologically weaker than these titles. In this book, "breviary" signifies the book used to pray the Liturgy of the Hours.

12. The fifth "hour" of the renewed Liturgy of the Hours—that is, the Office of Readings—may be prayed at any time of day. For monks, it remains linked to the late night or early morning hours.

13. Constitution on the Sacred Liturgy, *Sacrosanctum Concilium*, 100, in Austin Flannery, O.P., ed., *Vatican Council II: The Conciliar and Post Conciliar Documents* (Boston: St. Paul Editions, 1980), 28.

14. *General Instruction of the Liturgy of the Hours*, para. 27, in *The Liturgy of the Hours*, vol. 1, 36.

15. John Paul II, *Psalms and Canticles: Meditations and Catechesis on the Psalms and Canticles of Morning Prayer* (Chicago: Liturgical Training, 2004), 8.

16. Benedict XVI, address to general audience, St. Peter's Square, November 16, 2011, http://www.vatican.va/holy_father/benedict_xvi/audiences/2011/documents/hf_ben-xvi_aud_20111116_en.html. In this translation, the classic "Lauds," "Vespers," and "Compline" are used to render the Italian originals (*Lodi*, *Vespri*, and *Compieta*). I have changed these to the contemporary usage in English ("Morning Prayer," "Evening Prayer," and "Night Prayer").

17. *The Liturgy of the Hours*, vols. 1–4 (New York: Catholic Book, 1975–76).

18. Several verses of the psalms and three in their entirety (Psalms 58, 83, and 109) were omitted in the four-week psalter. These invoke God's vengeance on enemies in graphic language and so were judged difficult for the contemporary person.

19. The Catholic Book Publishing Company provides *Christian Prayer: The Liturgy of the Hours* (1976), a one-volume version of the Liturgy of the Hours with the complete texts of Morning, Evening, and Night Prayer for the entire year, as well as an abbreviated form of this volume titled *Shorter Christian Prayer* (1988), with the four-week psalter for Morning and Evening Prayer. Digital versions include *iBreviary* and *divineoffice.org*.

20. Paul VI, Apostolic Constitution *Laudis Canticum*, in *The Liturgy of the Hours*, vol. 1, 11.

21. Constitution on the Sacred Liturgy, *Sacrosanctum Concilium*, 83, in Flannery, *Vatican Council II*, 24.

22. RSVCE, second edition.

Chapter 1: Beginnings

1. *The Hours of the Divine Office in English and Latin* (Collegeville, MN: Liturgical, 1963).

2. In digital forms of the Liturgy of the Hours, all this is done for the user. There are no pages to find; one need only follow the Hour as given on the screen.

3. *Marialis Cultus* (Boston: Daughters of St. Paul, 1974), pp. 44–45, para. 53.

4. *General Instruction of the Liturgy of the Hours*, 27, quoted in *Marialis Cultus*, pp. 44–45, para. 53. Translation from *The Liturgy of the Hours*, vol. 1 (New York: Catholic Book, 1975), 36.

5. *Marialis Cultus*, p. 45, para. 53–54.

6. Ibid., p. 45, para. 54.

7. Among these are the Salve Regina (Hail, Holy Queen), Ave Maria (Hail Mary), Alma Redemptoris Mater (Loving Mother of the Redeemer), and so forth, as given at the conclusion of Night Prayer.

8. This was the Italian version (completed one year before the English version mentioned earlier): *Liturgia delle ore*, 4 vols. (Vatican: Tipografia Poliglotta Vaticana, 1974–75).

9. *General Instruction of the Liturgy of the Hours*, published at the beginning of *The Liturgy of the Hours*, vol. 1, 21–98. Also published by the United States Conference of Catholic Bishops, Washington, DC, 2009.

10. Vincenzo Raffa, P.O.D.P., *La liturgia delle ore: Presentazione storica, teologica, e pastorale* (Milano: Edizioni O.R., 1971). The first edition was published in 1971 and the second in 1972. It was one of these two shorter editions, published just a few years earlier, that I read. Father Raffa was the secretary of the General Commission for the renewal of the Divine Office. In the final section of this book, titled "For Further Reading," I have listed other works of value.

11. *The Liturgy of the Hours*, vol. 4, 723, 754, 966, 758.

12. Ibid., 1005, 1157, 1120.

13. International Commission on English in the Liturgy, *The Roman Pontifical* (Vatican City: Vatican Polyglot Press, 1978), 180–81.

14. Canon 276, § 2, 3, of the Code of Canon Law, states, "Priests as well as deacons aspiring to the priesthood are obliged to fulfill the Liturgy of the Hours daily in accordance with the proper

and approved liturgical books; permanent deacons, however, are to do the same to the extent it is determined by the conference of bishops." *Code of Canon Law: Latin-English Edition* (Washington, DC: Canon Law Society of America, 1983), 97. The United States Conference of Catholic Bishops adds, "Complementary Norm: Permanent deacons are required to include as part of their daily prayer those parts of the Liturgy of the Hours known as Morning and Evening Prayer. Permanent deacons are obliged to pray for the universal Church. Whenever possible, they should lead these prayers with the community to whom they have been assigned to minister." Posted on http://www.usccb.org/beliefs-and-teachings/ what-we-believe/canon-law/complementary-norms/canon-276-2-3 -priests-and-deacons-and-the-liturgy-of-the-hours.cfm.

Chapter 2: Questions

1. Constitution on the Sacred Liturgy, *Sacrosanctum Concilium*, 83, in Flannery, *Vatican Council II*, 24.

2. *General Instruction of the Liturgy of the Hours*, 29.

3. On *spiritual desolation* as Saint Ignatius of Loyola describes it, see note 4 of Chapter 3.

4. *General Instruction of the Liturgy of the Hours*, 115.

5. See *General Instruction of the Liturgy of the Hours*, 161–62, 250. The Spanish breviary, for example, includes the optional cycle of first readings.

6. Office of Readings, Holy Saturday, Second Reading, *The Liturgy of the Hours*, vol. 2, 497. The subsequent quotations are also from this source.

7. RNAB.

8. Morning Prayer, Friday, Third Week in Ordinary Time, *The Liturgy of the Hours*, vol. 3, 1089.

9. Office of Readings, January 25, Second Reading, *The Liturgy of the Hours*, vol. 3, 1322.

Chapter 3: Explorations

1. Scriptural quotation from RSVCE, second edition. See Mt 27:46.

2. *The Liturgy of the Hours*, vol. 1, 21–98.

3. *Spiritual Exercises*, 313–36.

4. Timothy Gallagher, O.M.V., *The Discernment of Spirits: An Ignatian Guide to Everyday Living* (New York: Crossroad, 2005). Ignatius gives the following examples of spiritual desolation: "darkness of soul, disturbance in it, movement to low and earthly

things, disquiet from various agitations and temptations, moving to lack of confidence, without hope, without love, finding oneself totally slothful, tepid, sad and, as if separated from one's Creator and Lord" (8).

5. Ignatius describes this tactic of the enemy in his first set of rules (*Spiritual Exercises*, 313–27).

6. Literally, "by insisting more upon prayer, meditation." Gallagher, *The Discernment of Spirits*, 8.

7. Office of Readings, February 23, Second Reading, *The Liturgy of the Hours*, vol. 2, 1695–96.

8. This is the "much examination" Ignatius counsels in rule 6: see Gallagher, *The Discernment of Spirits*, 8, 89–91.

9. A form of the classic examination of conscience that incorporates discernment of spirits into the prayer: see Timothy Gallagher, O.M.V., *The Examen Prayer: Ignatian Wisdom for Our Lives Today* (New York: Crossroad, 2006).

10. Night Prayer, Thursday, *The Liturgy of the Hours*, vol. 2, 1642–44.

11. Timothy Gallagher, O.M.V., *Meditation and Contemplation: An Ignatian Guide to Praying with Scripture* (New York: Crossroad, 2008). For the book on the examen prayer, see note 9 in this chapter.

12. *Spiritual Exercises*, 75. Author's translation.

13. RNAB.

14. Ibid.

15. See Gallagher, *The Examen Prayer*, 124.

16. RSVCE, second edition.

17. The Benedictine monk, Blessed Columba Marmion, writes, "Before reading the breviary it is a good thing to prepare our hearts to read it well. The first and most important point in this preparation is to spend a few moments in recollection. One cannot insist too much on this point. It is of capital importance. . . . You may be quite sure that the time devoted to preparation is not lost; on the contrary, these are golden minutes." Matthew Dillon, trans., *Christ—The Ideal of the Priest: Spiritual Conferences by the Right Rev. D. Columba Marmion* (St. Louis: B. Herder, 1953), 228, 230. The renewed Liturgy of the Hours proposes the following optional prayer before praying the Office alone: "Open, Lord, my mouth to bless your holy name; cleanse my heart from all empty, evil, or distracting thoughts; enlighten my mind, enkindle my heart, that I may recite this Office worthily, attentively, and devoutly, and may merit to be heard in the sight of your divine majesty. Through Christ Our Lord. Amen." Latin text in an insert to the Latin version: *Liturgia Horarum iuxta Ritum Romanum*, 4 vols. (Vatican City: Typis Polyglottis Vaticanis, 1977). Author's translation.

18. Office of Readings, Friday, First Week of Advent, Second Reading, *Proslogion*, in *The Liturgy of the Hours*, vol. 1, 184. I have translated "*homuncio*" as "little man" rather than "insignificant man" as found in the translation quoted.

19. Office of Readings, Friday, Sixth Week in Ordinary Time, Second Reading, *Tractates on the First Letter of John*, in *The Liturgy of the Hours*, vol. 3, 220.

20. Office of Readings, August 4, Second Reading, *Catechetical Instructions*, in *The Liturgy of the Hours*, vol. 3, 1573.

21. Office of Readings, November 1, Second Reading, *Sermon*, in *The Liturgy of the Hours*, vol. 4, 1526.

Chapter 4: Foundations

1. "Duties and obligations are merely the signposts which point out the road to some ultimate end in which our whole nature and its capacities are fulfilled. The fulfillment of an obligation does not, in itself, satisfy the aspirations of our being; but it brings us into contact with the One we seek. It unites us to God in a union of wills. And where the obligation is one of prayer, the union is more than a conformity of wills. Prayer demands intelligence. The Psalms bring our hearts and minds into the presence of the living God. They fill our minds with His Truth in order to unite us with His Love." Thomas Merton, *Bread in the Wilderness* (New York: New Directions, 1960), 13.

2. For the *General Instruction of the Liturgy of the Hours*, see note 9 in Chapter 1. For Father Vincenzo Raffa's book, see note 10 in Chapter 1. In the section titled "For Further Reading" in this book, I name other works of value.

3. Paul VI, Apostolic Constitution *Laudis Canticum*, in *The Liturgy of the Hours*, vol. 1, 11–20.

4. Ibid., 11.

5. *General Instruction of the Liturgy of the Hours*, 16.

6. Daytime Prayer, Thursday, Week Two, *The Liturgy of the Hours*, vol. 3, 928–29.

7. *General Instruction of the Liturgy of the Hours*, 155.

8. This *General Instruction* needs to be both *read* and *taught*. Many who pray the Liturgy of the Hours have the theological background necessary to read the *Instruction* fruitfully; all would benefit from hearing it taught or exploring it in groups.

9. A.-M. Roguet, O.P., *The Liturgy of the Hours: The General Instruction on the Liturgy of the Hours with a Commentary* (Collegeville, MN: Liturgical Abbey, 1971), 82.

10. Monday, Week Two of the Psalter, hymn for Morning Prayer, *The Liturgy of the Hours*, vol. 3, 851; Saturday, Week Two

of the Psalter, hymn for the Office of Readings, *The Liturgy of the Hours*, vol. 3, 958.

11. Thursday, Week One of the Psalter, Evening Prayer, *The Liturgy of the Hours*, vol. 3, 780; Sunday, Week Three of the Psalter, Morning Prayer, *The Liturgy of the Hours*, vol. 3, 985; Sunday, Week One of the Psalter, Evening Prayer, *The Liturgy of the Hours*, vol. 3, 699.

12. *The Liturgy of the Hours*, vol. 3, 656, 669.

13. A.-M. Roguet, *The Liturgy of the Hours*, 81–82, also helped me realize that for Ignatius of Loyola, praise is the primary purpose of the human person. In his classic Principle and Foundation (*Spiritual Exercises*, no. 23), Ignatius writes, "Man is created to *praise*, reverence, and serve God our Lord." Emphasis added.

14. Hymns for Night Prayer, *The Liturgy of the Hours*, vol. 3, 1264.

15. Baptism of the Lord, *The Liturgy of the Hours*, vol. 1, 630.

16. Monday, Week One of the Psalter, Morning Prayer, *The Liturgy of the Hours*, vol. 3, 709; Friday, Week One of the Psalter, Morning Prayer, *The Liturgy of the Hours*, vol. 3, 791.

17. Sunday, Week Three of the Psalter, Evening Prayer One, *The Liturgy of the Hours*, vol. 3, 975.

18. "The person who prays the psalms in the name of the Church should be aware of their total meaning (*sensus plenus*), especially their messianic meaning, which was the reason for the Church's introduction of the psalter into its prayer. This messianic meaning was fully revealed in the New Testament and indeed was publicly acknowledged by Christ the Lord in person when he said to the apostles: 'All that is written about me in the law of Moses and the prophets and the psalms must be fulfilled' (Luke 24:44). The best known example of this messianic meaning is the dialogue in Matthew's Gospel on the Messiah as Son of David and David's Lord: there, psalm 110 is interpreted as messianic. Following this line of thought, the Fathers of the Church saw the whole psalter as a prophecy of Christ and the Church and explained it in this sense; for the same reason the Psalms have been chosen for use in the sacred liturgy." *General Instruction*, 109, in *The Liturgy of the Hours*, vol. 1, 59.

19. Sunday, Week One of the Psalter, Morning Prayer, *The Liturgy of the Hours*, vol. 3, 688.

20. Tuesday, Week Four of the Psalter, Evening Prayer, *The Liturgy of the Hours*, vol. 3, 1181.

21. John Brook, *The School of Prayer: An Introduction to the Divine Office for All Christians* (Collegeville, MN: Liturgical, 1992), 401. This is a fine resource for praying the psalms.

22. RSVCE, second edition.

23. *Discourse on Psalm 85*, quoted in *General Instruction of the Liturgy of the Hours*, 7.

24. Dogmatic Constitution on the Church, *Lumen Gentium*, 11, in Flannery, *Vatican Council II*, 362.

25. *General Instruction*, 12, in *The Liturgy of the Hours*, vol. 1, 29.

26. Daniel de Reynal, *Théologie de la Liturgie des Heures* (Paris: Éditions Beauchesne, 1978), 28.

Chapter 5: Journey

1. Quoted with permission.

2. Quoted with permission.

3. Father Eugène Hains, quoted in Henri de Lubac, S.J., *At the Service of the Church: Henri de Lubac Reflects on the Circumstances That Occasioned His Writings* (San Francisco: Ignatius, 1993), 402.

4. Quotations from the materials provided for those who wished to join the monks in prayer.

5. RNAB.

6. For a layperson's perspective on how the Liturgy of the Hours may be prayed in the lay vocation, see Daria Sockey, *The Everyday Catholic's Guide to the Liturgy of the Hours* (Cincinnati: Servant, 2013). The availability of the Liturgy of the Hours online and through mobile applications has greatly expanded access to it and the settings in which it may be prayed.

CROSSROAD

You Might Also Like

Timothy M. Gallagher, O.M.V.
BEGIN AGAIN
The Life and Spiritual Legacy of Bruno Lanteri
Paperback, 329 pages, ISBN 978-08245-25798
Also available as an e-book

Father Gallagher assembles a remarkable biography of Father Bruno Lanteri (1759–1830), who, while living in a context of exciting historical significance, overcame great odds to become a primary spiritual leader in his age.

"Bruno Lanteri personally experienced God as a Father who loves and forgives, and so, throughout a lifetime of intensely active ministry, he became an apostle of God's mercy, in particular toward those who struggled spiritually."
—Fr. Louis Normandin, O.M.V., member of the General Council in the Oblates of the Virgin Mary

Support your local bookstore or order directly from the publisher at www.CrossroadPublishing.com.

To request a catalog or inquire about quantity orders, please e-mail sales@CrossroadPublishing.com.

CROSSROAD

Father Gallagher's
Popular Titles Available as Audio Books

Timothy M. Gallagher, O.M.V.
THE DISCERNMENT OF SPIRITS
An Ignatian Guide for Everyday Living
Read by Daniel P. Barron, O.M.V.
CD, 9 hours, ISBN 978-08245-20045

St. Ignatius Loyola, founder of the Jesuits, is one of the most influential spiritual leaders of all time, yet many readers find his Rules for Discernment hard to understand. What can Ignatius teach us about the discernment of spirits that lies at the very heart of Christian life? In *The Discernment of Spirits*, talented teacher, retreat leader, and scholar Timothy M. Gallagher helps us understand the Rules and how their insights are essential for our spiritual growth today.

DISCERNING THE WILL OF GOD
An Ignatian Guide to Christian Decision Making
Read by John Wykes, O.M.V.
CD, 5 hours, ISBN 978-08245-20274

For everyone ready to make the shift from "What do I want for my life?" to "What does God want for my life?" Father Timothy Gallagher offers guidance to help you make sense of your major life decisions. Drawing from the timeless methods of Ignatius Loyola and richly illustrated with examples and stories, this audiobook offers practical wisdom for aligning your will to God's will.

Support your local bookstore or order directly from
the publisher at www.CrossroadPublishing.com.

To request a catalog or inquire about quantity orders,
please e-mail sales@CrossroadPublishing.com.

CROSSROAD

Titles on Ignatian Spirituality
Timothy M. Gallagher, O.M.V.

Over one hundred thousand readers have turned to Fr. Gallagher's Ignatian titles for reliable, inspirational, and clear explanations of some of the most important aspects of Christian spirituality. Whether you're a spiritual director, priest, minister, longtime spiritual seeker, or beginner, Fr. Gallagher's books have much to offer you in different moments in life.

- When you need short, practical exercises for young and old: *An Ignatian Introduction to Prayer*

  Group leaders who are looking for practical exercises for groups—including groups who may not have much experience in spiritual development—will want to acquire *An Ignatian Introduction to Prayer: Scriptural Reflections According to the Spiritual Exercises*. This book features forty short (two-page) Ignatian meditations, including Scripture passages, meditative keys for entering into the scriptural story, and guided questions for reflection. These exercises are also useful for individual reflection for both experienced persons and beginners: beginners will recognize and resonate with some of the evocative passages from Scripture; those familiar with Ignatian teaching will appreciate the Ignatian structure of the guided questions.

- When your life is at the crossroads: *Discerning the Will of God*

  If you are facing a turning point in life, you know how difficult it can be to try to hear God's will amid the noise of other people's expectations and your own wishes. Ignatius of Loyola developed a series of exercises and reflections designed to help you in these times so that your decision can be one that conforms to God's will for your life. *Discerning the Will of God: An Ignatian Guide to Christian Decision Making* is a trustworthy guide to applying those

CROSSROAD

reflections to your own particular circumstances. This guide, which does not require any prior knowledge of Ignatian spirituality, can be used by people of any faith, though some elements will be more directly applicable to Catholic readers.

- When you want classic spiritual discipline to apply every day: *The Examen Prayer* and *Meditation and Contemplation*

    Individuals wanting to deepen their prayer lives using a spiritual discipline will find *The Examen Prayer* an important resource. The examen prayer is a powerful and increasingly popular resource for finding God's hand in our everyday lives and learning to be receptive to God's blessings. This easy-to-read book uses stories and examples to explain what the examen is, how you can begin to pray it, how you can adapt it to your individual life, and what its benefits for your life can be. It is highly practical!

    Because *The Examen Prayer* draws from the experiences of everyday life, it can stand on its own as a guide to the prayer of examen. Those looking to begin their practice of meditation and contemplation, which for Ignatius is always based on Scripture, may choose their own Scripture passages or draw from the forty examples in *An Ignatian Introduction to Prayer,* mentioned earlier.

    A second favorite is *Meditation and Contemplation: An Ignatian Guide to Praying with Scripture.* Anyone familiar with Ignatian spirituality has heard about meditation and contemplation. In this volume, Fr. Gallagher explains what is unique to each practice, shows how you can profit from both at different times in your spiritual life, and reveals some of the forgotten elements (such as the preparatory steps and colloquy) and how the structure can be adapted to your particular spiritual needs.

- When you're ready to move more deeply into Ignatian thought: *The Discernment of Spirits* and *Spiritual Consolation*

CROSSROAD

Spiritual directors, directees, and others who want to understand the deeper structures of Ignatian thought have come to rely on *The Discernment of Spirits: An Ignatian Guide to Everyday Living* and *Spiritual Consolation: An Ignatian Guide for the Greater Discernment of Spirits*. *The Discernment of Spirits* leads us through Ignatius's rules for discernment, showing both their precise insight into the human soul and their ability to illustrate the real-life struggles of spiritual seekers today. As Fr. Gallagher writes, his practical goal is "to offer an experience-based presentation of Ignatius's rules for discernment of spirits in order to facilitate their ongoing application in the spiritual life. This is a book about living the spiritual life." Because it forms the foundation for so many other aspects of Ignatian thought, *The Discernment of Spirits* has become Fr. Gallagher's best-selling book and has been the basis for a TV series.

Spiritual Consolation extends this same approach, interweaving stories and principles for a more profound understanding of Ignatius's Second Rules for Discernment.

CROSSROAD

About the Author

Father Timothy M. Gallagher, O.M.V. (frtimothygallagher.org), was ordained in 1979 as a member of the Oblates of the Virgin Mary, a religious community dedicated to retreats and spiritual formation according to the Spiritual Exercises of Saint Ignatius. He obtained his doctorate in 1983 from the Gregorian University. He has taught (St. John's Seminary, Brighton, MA; Our Lady of Grace Seminary Residence, Boston, MA), assisted in formation work for twelve years, and served two terms as provincial in his own community. He has dedicated many years to an extensive ministry of retreats, spiritual direction, and teaching about the spiritual life. Fr. Gallagher is the author of nine books (Crossroad) on the spiritual teaching of Saint Ignatius of Loyola and the life of Venerable Bruno Lanteri, founder of the Oblates of the Virgin Mary.

About the Publisher

The Crossroad Publishing Company publishes CROSS-ROAD and HERDER & HERDER books. We offer a 200-year global family tradition of books on spiritual living and religious thought. We promote reading as a time-tested discipline for focus and understanding. We help authors shape, clarify, write, and effectively promote their ideas. We select, edit, and distribute books. Our expertise and passion is to provide wholesome spiritual nourishment for heart, mind, and soul through the written word.